The Gentle Art of
GETTING YOUR OWN WAY

Proven ways to help you get agreement
at work and at home

Patrick Forsyth

foulsham

LONDON • NEW YORK • TORONTO • SYDNEY

foulsham

The Publishing House, Bennetts Close, Cippenham,
Slough, Berkshire, SL1 5AP, England

Foulsham books can be found in all good bookshops and direct
from www.foulsham.com

ISBN 978-0-572-03322-4

Printed in Great Britain by Creative Print & Design (Wales), Ebbw Vale

Acknowledgements

Ability is the art of getting credit for all the home runs somebody else hits.

George Graham
Football player and manager

I would like to thank fellow author Frances Kay for prompting my initial meeting with Foulsham. When we crossed paths at the London Book Fair, she persuaded me that I should walk a little further and that I did not need another cup of tea just yet, but that we should first visit one more stand. So a little successful persuasion initiated the events that led to this book being written.

So too did a career in management training and consultancy, and I am grateful to all the many people – colleagues, collaborators and clients – who have assisted me with the constant learning process that is essential in such a field, and which have made it possible for me to comment on such matters as I do here. Early in my career I had an involvement in selling and later, having moved into training, conducted many courses on aspects of sales technique; indeed, I continue to do so. I have also written on the subject. As there are many other circumstances in which persuasion is necessary, I am delighted to have had the opportunity to present something of these techniques in a way that makes them generally applicable.

Authors tend to think writing is the be all and end all of the process of producing a book. Not so: there is so much more to be done and many people are involved in doing it. Thanks are due therefore to Wendy Hobson and her colleagues at Foulsham. I try not to be a prima donna as an author and not to make the jobs of such people harder than they already are. From my standpoint, you are certainly all a pleasure to work with; now go persuade people to buy this!

Most people do not admit they engage in selling …
*But if you are pursuing power, you are selling
almost all the time.*

Thomas L. Quick
Author of training books

About the author

Given the topic of this book it is perhaps appropriate to mention the author's credentials in offering advice in this area. Patrick Forsyth runs *Touchstone Training & Consultancy*, an independent firm specialising in the improvement of business performance, and focusing primarily on marketing, sales, communications and management skills.

As a consultant and trainer of more than 25 years' experience, Patrick has fronted a great variety of events and as a trainer he has led countless management training courses on aspects of marketing, including sales and other communications skills. Many of these have been for individual companies and others take the form of public seminars for organisations such as The Institute of Management (and similar bodies overseas, for example, The Singapore Institute of Management). He has also spoken at many conferences, some public events, some for specialist bodies such as Central Law Training and others for individual organisations.

His training work has always included many workshops designed to develop participants' skills in persuasive communication and selling. In addition, among a number of successful books that he has written, two are on the topic of selling in a business context: *The Sales Excellence Pocketbook* (Management Pocketbooks) and *100 Great Sales Ideas* (Cyan Books), as have been many published articles. His books now cover more than business topics and recent additions include humour (*Surviving in the Office Jungle*), and travel writing (*First class – at last!* a light-hearted account of a rail journey from Singapore to Bangkok); both published by Marshall Cavendish.

He began his career in publishing and, having failed to become managing editor in the first six months, moved into selling and then marketing. Since moving into consultancy, selling has always been a necessary stock in trade; clients do not very often arrive unbidden waving cheques and saying, *Start work now!* They need to be persuaded that doing so makes sense. This book only came about after several discussions and two different versions of the proposal! So too in other aspects of life, he has needed to be persuasive in meetings, on committees and, while he does not always get his own way (certainly with his family!), he likes to feel he achieves a good strike rate.

He has another book published by Foulsham: *How to craft successful business presentations and effective public speaking.* Given a chance, he will persuade you to buy a copy of it.

Patrick Forsyth
Touchstone Training & Consultancy
28 Saltcote Maltings
Maldon
Essex
CM9 4QP
United Kingdom
Telephone and Fax: +44 (0)1621 859300
E-mail: patrick@touchstonetc.freeserve.co.uk

Contents

Preface

I am not arguing with you –
I am telling you.

James Whistler
Painter and etcher

Consider how viewpoints differ. First, assume you are standing reading this in a bookshop. I want you to buy this book. Why? Well, from my standpoint, because if you, and a sufficient number of other people, do buy it then I will make some money. So, go on – buy it. So far I am probably only succeeding in putting you off. I cannot just *tell* you to buy it, and expect you to do so just to please me. I have to give you a reason. Well, it is not expensive, its length means you will not need to tie up an inordinate amount of time reading it, it fits in your pocket and the cover is tastefully designed and a nice colour.

This is not much better. These are reasons of a sort to buy, but they are subsidiary to the larger issue of what the content of the book is and whether it would actually be useful to you. Start again. Think about communication for a moment. It can be difficult. The world is full of communications that are unclear – *you fit the thingy into the whatsit and* ... (just try it). Or imprecise – *...go straight on for about a mile* ... (three miles later ...). Communication can be made impossible to penetrate by jargon (like calling a spade a manual excavation device), by gobbledygook or, in a work context, by 'officespeak' (over-formalised business language). All such things can make understanding even more difficult. The confusion that can often result may be minor, or it may cause major problems. And things get even more complicated when you want to get someone to do something – when you seek to *persuade*. In most circumstances, and certainly in the work environment, just saying *do it* is not enough. It can raise eyebrows, hackles or temperatures – or all three. Persuasion is not about finding a way of forcing someone to do what you want; it is about getting your own way by making someone feel that doing as you suggest is the right course of action for them also.

Everyone spends a major part of their time communicating at work, socially and in all the many interactions they have with other people – and much of that communication is also designed to be persuasive. So, let's go back to this book: given that it is about making communication persuasive, will you buy it? The answer may still be negative. But consider: how about if the book will help you get your own way more certainly and more often? If it will reduce the frictions of communications breakdowns at home and at work; help you be seen as a clear, authoritative communicator; and if you are reminded of how agreements you do make can help you save time, save money and … but we are getting ahead of ourselves. Persuasion needs to provide reasons for action, and I am now offering reasons to buy that affect *you*. But you cannot gain all this just by reading a couple of pages in the bookshop. You do actually need to read it all; but given those last reasons, now will you buy it? After all, if I can make you do what I want and buy a copy – perhaps I can help you to get others to do what you want. It is worth thinking about.

Patrick Forsyth

Introduction: First Steps

> *One should not aim at being possible to understand,*
> *but at being impossible to misunderstand.*

Marcus Fabius Quintilian
Roman rhetorician

I try to practise what I preach, so, in writing about communication let me aim to be clear. This book is about creating and maximising communication success. It presents powerful methods, concepts and techniques designed to win agreement and prompt action from other people.

In straightforward terms it sets out to:

- •)) Demonstrate the nature of communicating persuasively, and show how it can be approached successfully and how any difficulties can be overcome.

- •)) Review the techniques of persuasive communication and focus on key aspects of the process in which the right approach makes being successful more likely.

- •)) Highlight techniques to differentiate you from other people and allow you to create a powerful case.

The ideas are presented in an accessible way that links easily to many everyday situations, with techniques being valid in both work and non-work situations.

If getting your own way is to be possible – or at least made more likely – then you need to gain agreement from other people. Doing so is not about blackmail or brute force; we want people to go along with our ideas willingly. This is not easy. This book would be much shorter if there was some straightforward magic formula, a wand that you could simply wave and guarantee agreement with your every idea. Some ideas find easy agreement; in other instances, agreement may be difficult and sometimes impossible to achieve.

If I tried to persuade you to put your hand in boiling water, no argument is likely to persuade you to do so. Yet if you have read this far then it may well mean that something persuaded you to buy this book. Persuasion may not be easy, but often it is possible. There may be no magic formula, but there are principles and approaches that make a message persuasive, and if you deploy these you are more likely to be successful.

These techniques are not themselves complicated. By and large they are pretty much common sense (otherwise I probably could not write about them!). The complexity comes in orchestrating the process in a way that deploys the techniques appropriately into a flowing conversation. Your final chosen approach must be acceptable to the other person and yet also present a persuasive case – one that prompts agreement.

The detail matters here. As we will see, small changes to how an argument is put over can make all the difference, turning a *yes* into a *no*, or vice versa. We start, at what may seem a step back from persuasiveness, with basic communication itself; although, as we will see, 'basic' is perhaps the wrong word and misunderstandings abound. No one agrees to something they do not understand (well, not often, and leaving my mobile phone contract on one side), so clarity of communication is the foundation upon which persuasion can be built. And clarity can be a challenge to achieve.

Inherent difficulties

Recognising that communications is never easy is the first step to making your communications successful. Before you have any hope of persuading, you must get people's attention and you must make them understand the meaning of what you say. As was said in the preface, communications breakdowns abound. Homes and offices throughout the land are ringing with voices at this very moment saying: *If you meant that, why didn't you say so? – But you never said that – Oh, I see – What?* – and more. All of us have found ourselves getting angry with someone – *What's the matter with this idiot, don't they understand anything?* – when what is actually at fault may be the clarity of our own communication (be honest!).

Why does this happen? There are a number of specific reasons and, more important, also a number of ways of acting to get over these inherent problems. So, leave what makes a message persuasive on one side for a moment and consider its clarity.

The problem is people do not listen, find it difficult to understand, are reluctant to agree or act and make things more difficult by providing inaccurate or inadequate feedback. Consider the following in turn.

Paying attention

People find it difficult to listen (or to concentrate on reading for that matter), certainly for any length of time. Long monologues are resented, and something like this book falls into many sections and uses many headings to provide breaks and stop it being seen as (and looking) difficult to access. In addition, people are selective. They pay attention to what *seems to them* to be important and may make the wrong assumptions about what are, in fact, the key parts of a message.

The moral: you always have to work hard at making sure your message really is taken in.

Understanding

There are a number of natural human reactions that act to dilute understanding. People always make assumptions based on their past experience – *sounds a bit like ... to me*. If you do not take that into account there can be no frame of reference to which your message can link. This is one of the reasons communication across age or gender gaps can cause problems.

For instance, jargon can be a problem. It may provide a convenient form of shorthand between people in the know, but can confuse others. Think of the now ubiquitous 'computerspeak', of things abbreviated to sets of initials like DUIU (Don't Use Initials Unnecessarily) and of many terms technical to some and second nature to others. Further, people are reluctant to say that they do not understand something in case this makes them look stupid.

In addition, assumptions are often made before someone even finishes what they are saying, as people say to themselves – *I know where this is going*. At that point their mind stops concentrating on listening and spends more effort on planning a response. This situation is compounded if conversation is heated for any reason – *I know where this is going and I don't like it*. Logic goes out the window, emotion may take over and, at worst, the conversation deteriorates into a ping-pong match of insults (*Don't talk while I'm interrupting!*) that can usually achieve nothing.

Things spoken but not seen may be more easily misunderstood. Thus showing things may be useful; so too is a message that 'paints a picture'.

The moral: expect achieving understanding to need care.

Agreeing

This takes us further towards persuasion. People are often suspicious of those with 'something to sell'. If agreeing to something might leave them open to being shown to be wrong, and thus involves an element of risk, that too can push people away from agreement.

The moral: even a strong case, which logic dictates should be accepted, may be resisted.

Taking action

Deciding to take action may mean someone has to change a habit (perhaps of a lifetime!). Considering taking action also gets people considering the risk – *If I do this and it doesn't work out, what then?* – and some people simply find decision-making hard and will sit on the fence forever if they can. All this can prevent persuasiveness working, or at least make it more difficult to get your own way.

The moral: even when the argument seems to have been accepted and there is no logical reason not to act, you need to recognise that it may take something more to actually prompt someone into action.

Obtaining feedback

People are not always open in communication. They may hide their feelings, intentionally or for other reasons (for example out of embarrassment), or what they do offer by way of feedback may be difficult to interpret.

The moral: feedback needs to be teased out, and it must never be forgotten that appearances can be deceptive.

All this begins to explain some of the difficulties that communications regularly produces. The first job is simply to recognise and remember the likely problems. If you *expect* difficulties in these kinds of ways, then that is the first step to getting over them. There is help at hand, however, because other inherent factors about the nature of communication can act to assist in making it successful; again the trick is to know what these things are, and to use them appropriately.

Aids to understanding

The four factors now mentioned (stemming from what psychologists call the 'laws of learning') all provide assistance to the process. They can be described as follows.

Addressing the individual's questions

(This is what psychologists call the law of effect.) What is people's first response to any message? They ask about its effect on *them*. They want to know if it will affect them, and if so whether the effects will be positive or negative. This is surely easy enough to understand; it is what we all do ourselves. Knowing this, we can include something about any effects within the message, addressing the problem rather than leaving a host of questions floating in the air.

This may often be as simple as the difference between saying to someone – *do this and productivity will be improved* – and saying something like – *do this and your workload will be easier to cope with, you will have more time to concentrate on priorities and productivity will increase.*

Making it logical (or Forward association)

This is no more than choosing to go through things in a logical order (and perhaps explaining what that order is). Information is better retained in the order in which it is taken in. If we have to re-sort it, something may be lost in the process. Consider something like your telephone number. You know it backwards. Well do you? You certainly know it forwards, but if you try to recite it backwards this involves a recognisably different thinking process and probably takes a moment longer (try it).

So, give people things in the right order, no sorting is then necessary and they can consider and use the information more easily. If your message comes over in random bits – *and another thing ...* – it will never be so powerful.

Linking to experience (or Belonging)

Whatever anyone says to anyone else is considered in the light of his or her prior experience. Phone a supplier to check some detail of your account and consider what goes through your mind if they say – *I'll need to check with the computer.* Perhaps this creates a vision of instant efficiency and good service – perhaps not. It depends on what prior experiences with computer systems come to mind; and I know what comes to *my* mind!

The same kind of response always happens. If you link accurately to people's experience, understanding is easier; if you misjudge what they know already or assume they have experiences that in fact they do not have, confusion can result. Specific linking – *this will be like the meeting we had to discuss …* – with someone calling up an image of a constructive two-hour meeting that they remember really got some new ideas on the go, makes what follows that much easier.

Repeating (or Repetition)

Any message, especially a complex one, may be better taken in if it is repeated. Any message, especially a complex one … no, that does not mean simply repeating the same words again and again. It means that finding acceptable ways to repeat key parts of a message can be a useful way to reinforce understanding.

Considering a number of examples makes this clear (and adding an example is itself just a way of introducing one element of repetition). A meeting followed by the issue of minutes of the proceedings is repetition. Something said and demonstrated, or illustrated by a visual aid, is repetition. So too is something that acts to summarise. As is crosschecking and using more than one form of words – *that's important, let me put it another way.* You can probably think of more examples, and may well be conscious of doing this yourself in various ways already. Deploying repetition as an intentional technique can strengthen understanding and avoid avoidable misunderstanding.

Deploying repetition as an intentional technique – sorry, enough: point made.

The overall message here is simple, but it has a plethora of implications. Communication can be inherently difficult. It works best if we understand what difficulties are most likely to arise, and why, and if we utilise other inherent aspects of the communications process to assist getting our message over accurately and smoothly.

Understanding, and therefore clarity, is the foundation of persuasion. No one is going to agree and take the action you want if they do not know, or are not sure, what it is. With that in mind we can move on to approaches and techniques that will specifically help you to get your own way. The degree of complexity explored to date already implies that this does not just happen.

Clarity is one thing, but what factors actually make even a clear message persuasive? The first step in creating such a message is to understand something of how they are received. It is to this that we turn next.

Clear, well-considered communication provides a sound foundation for anyone wanting to be persuasive. It avoids misunderstandings and others may well appreciate the clarity of it: it can enhance the profile of the communicator in a way that impresses and can certainly act to increase the likelihood of ultimate success in getting your own way.

CHAPTER 1

The Concept of 'Helping People to Decide'

I persuade, you educate, they manipulate.

Dr Allen Crawford
Author

There is a danger that persuasion is undertaken without sufficient care. It can seem easy: after all, if you know what you are suggesting, and it is good, surely all you have to do is tell people about it? Not so, as we will see. For example, the Chairperson of a committee might, intent on conducting an orderly and effective meeting, want to sell people on sticking strictly to a published agenda. Sensible enough surely, but a brief request simply to do so may still prompt argument. Why? Because with no reasons given, people may draw the wrong conclusions: *It will curtail what I have to say, it will stop us dealing with X.* They may react in a hundred and one different ways – all of which may go against what the Chairperson really wants to achieve. Matters may work out to be worse still if they were condescending too, or in any way inappropriately abrupt or demanding.

This danger is a very real one too, and disaster is almost guaranteed if you take the wrong view of the persuasion process. This is not something you can regard as something you 'do to people'. That makes the process seem inappropriately one way, when it should be a dialogue.

The best definition I know of selling is that it is *helping people to buy*. Similarly, in non-sales situations, persuasion is well described as *helping people to make a decision*.

This may seem simplistic, but it does characterise the reality of the process well. People want to go through a process of decision making;

indeed, they will do just that whatever you may do. So, the core of what makes the basis for persuasive technique is a two-way process and both elements start on the other person's side of the relationship. Always, you must consider the way in which people assess something and make a decision. Those buying products and services illustrate what goes on: they investigate options and weigh up the pros and cons of any given case (and often, of course, they are intentionally checking out several competing options alongside one another); just as you do when you set out to buy a new TV or washing machine.

Whatever decision they are faced with, how do people make a choice? They go through a particular sequence of thinking. One way of looking at this, defined by psychologists way back, is paraphrased here (see boxed paragraph on page 21). People are likely to do the following:

- •)) Consider the factors that make up a case.

- •)) Seek to categorise these as advantages or disadvantages.

- •)) Weigh up the complete case, allowing for all the pluses and minuses.

- •)) Select a course of action (which may be simply agreeing or not, or involve the choice of one action being taken rather than another or a choice being made from several options), which they conclude reflects the overall picture.

Let us be clear. What is going on here is not a search for perfection. Most things we look at have some downsides: this may be the most useful book you have ever read, but reading it does take a little time, and that time could be used for something else. This time disappearing might well be seen as a downside. The analogy of a set of weighing scales, with each side containing pluses and minuses of differing weight, is worth keeping in mind (see Figure 1 on page 22).

This analogy can act as a practical tool, helping you envisage what is going on during what you intend to be a persuasive exchange. Beyond that it helps structure the process if you also have a clear idea of the sequence of thinking people involve in their weighing-up process.

The thinking process

One way to look at what is going on is to think of people moving through several stages of thinking, and possibly saying to themselves:

- •)) **I matter most.** Whatever you want me to do, I expect you to worry about how I feel about it, respect me and consider my situation and needs.

- •)) **What are the merits and implications of the case you make?** Tell me what you suggest and why it makes sense (the pluses) and whether it has any snags (the minuses) so that I can weigh it up; bearing in mind that few, if any, propositions are perfect.

- •)) **How will it work?** Here people additionally want to assess the details not so much about the proposition itself, but about the areas associated with it. For example, you might want to persuade someone to take on, or become involved with, a project. The idea of the project might appeal, but say it ends with them having to prepare a lengthy written report, they might see that as a chore and therefore as a minus and might, if the case is finely balanced, reject it because of that.

- •)) **What do I do?** In other words, what action – exactly – is now necessary? This too forms part of the balance. If something seen in a quick flick through this book persuaded you that it might help you, you may have bought it because of that. In doing so you recognised (and accepted) that you would have to read it and that this would take a little time. The action – reading – is inherent in the proposition and, if you were not prepared to take it on, this might have changed your decision.

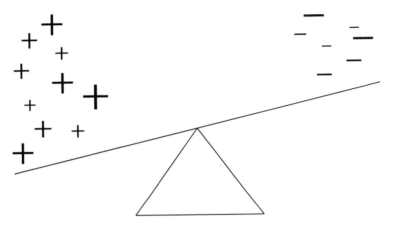

Figure 1: 'Weighing up the decision'

Once this thinking is complete people will feel they have sufficient evidence on which to make a decision. They have the balance in mind, and they can compare it with that of any other options (and remember, some choices are close run with one option only just coming out ahead of others). Then people can decide; and feel they have made a sensible decision, and that they have done so on a suitably considered basis.

This thinking process is largely universal. Depending on what is being done, it may happen very quickly and might even be almost instantaneous – the classic snap judgement. Or it may take longer, and that may sometimes indicate days or weeks (or longer!) rather than minutes or hours. But it is *always* in evidence. Because of this, there is always merit in setting out your case in a way that sits comfortably alongside the way in which it will be considered: hence, the definition that describes persuasion as *helping the decision-making process*.

Thus this thinking process should not be difficult to identify with because it is what you do too. Witness the purchase of a television mentioned earlier. Essentially all that is necessary when attempting to persuade is to keep this process in mind, and address the individual questions involved in turn. Thus you need to:

- ·))) **Start by demonstrating a focus on the other person:** it helps also to aim to create some rapport and make clear how you aim to put things over (making clear, for example, in what sequence you plan to go through things).

- ·))) **Present a balanced case:** you need to stress the positive, of course, but should not pretend there are no snags, especially if manifestly there are some. So you must present a clear case, give it sufficient explanation and weight and recognise the balancing up that the recipient will undertake in their mind.

- ·))) **Add in working details:** mention how things will work; include ancillary details, especially those that will matter to others.

In this way, when you set out a case the structure and logic of it should sensibly follow this pattern. Otherwise the danger is that you will be trying to do one thing while the person you are communicating with is doing something else; and they will surely do what *they* want.

Each step in the process must be taken before people will willingly move on to the next one. Some decisions can be taken at once while others require a pause between each stage. The core of this process is that we weigh up the pros and cons of making a decision. We all want to be able to make an appropriately informed decision; we put different points on one side of the metaphorical balance or on the other. Nothing is perfect, so what wins is best thought of as what has the most positive balance. Thus in competitive situations a case can be won, or lost, on the basis of just one or two small points swinging the balance one way or another.

The science of persuasion

The process and psychology described here was first set out in this sort of form in the 1960s. During the ensuing years these or similar principles have been the basis of much communications teaching and of personal skills training in the business world, and always it has made good sense, while only being essentially an observation of 'what seemed to be the case'.

As one who has conducted umpteen sales training courses over the years and said much in them based on this kind of thinking, I was pleased to see these principles take a firm step towards scientific validation quite recently. In the magazine *Scientific American Mind* (Volume 14, number 1) the article 'The Science of Persuasion: social psychology has determined the basic principles that govern getting to 'yes'' by Robert B Cialdini, Regents' Professor of Psychology at Arizona State University, set out a case for being persuasive that parallels these 'well-known' business principles very closely. So, if you want the science bit, get yourself a back issue. If you just want to be persuasive, read on. While not everything psychologists do is practical (I am reminded of the definition of a psychologist as a sex maniac who failed the practical), this is all based very much on an examination of what works.

The process of making most decisions always follows this multi-stage process. But execution of the process can be complex and reflects the circumstances of the decision making. (In selling it might reflect the nature of the customer's business; the size of their organisation; the people and functions involved; their needs, and the degree of influence they have on buying decisions – and what they are buying.) As an example, an organisation considering with whom to commission a major research study is likely to go through a more complex process than that of an individual deciding where to get their car serviced. Everything persuasive is best viewed from this perspective. As has been said, it is not something that you do *to* people: it is the mirror image of the decision-making process – something that is inherently two way.

Persuasion is, to a considerable extent, a process of need satisfaction and research shows two facts that are extremely valuable. First, that communications are much more successful when a person's situation is clearly identified. And, conversely, they are less successful when such information is only implied (in effect, guessed), or is ignored. Asking the right questions is thus as important to being successfully persuasive as saying the right things is (more of this anon).

Nothing is successfully agreed unless someone *willingly* agrees. There may be some reluctance, but if people feel their arms have been twisted too much they resent it and this can affect the action they then take; at worst, they may renege on their commitment. There is a need to relate closely what is done in communicating persuasively to others' points of view; this can only be done if what you say is thought through carefully. Your approach must therefore be, in a word: planned (something we turn to in the next chapter).

To get your own way you must be in the business of playing a part in other people's decision-making processes, assisting them to make decisions – the right ones – rather than pressurising them into doing something against their better judgement. You must sometimes play the role, in part, of an advisor; and being regarded as an advisor simply does not fit with a high-pressure approach.

If the right approach is adopted and accepted, agreement is more likely to be reached.

With that in mind we turn to the complete process involved in what we might call a persuasive encounter.

The structure of the task

The actual task facing you here can be seen as spanning a number of stages. Some of these will be dealt with individually later in the book. Here let's get them in perspective:

- •)) **Planning:** With someone in mind, and a conversation or meeting in prospect, some preparation is often necessary. The most persuasive people do not just 'wing it'; they create an approach tailored to achieve their aims and matched to each particular person they aim to persuade. At its simplest this is no more than adhering to the old adage to *engage the brain before the mouth.*

- •)) **Handling the conversation/meeting:** When a formal (or indeed less formal) meeting is involved, it needs approaching systematically. A meeting needs some structure and must be designed to take an amount of time acceptable to the other party. The plan is like a route map, as important to assist when it is not possible to follow the planned route, as it is when you can. The course of a meeting cannot be dictated; it must follow to some degree the events that occur and what is said even though you will want to keep it as much as possible on *your* track.

In thinking through the best approach, it helps to consider the logical stages of a meeting.

- •)) **Opening:** The first moments, making a good first impression, if necessary identifying something about the other person and their situation and setting the scene for the way you want to describe your offering.

- •)) **Presentation:** Making your case, and putting it across in a way that ensures that it can act persuasively. How this is done, the power and precision of your description and more are vital to success.

- •)) **Handling objections:** Any pitch is likely to give rise to some objections – the 'buts' (which may in any case only be clarifying questions) – and this stage too must be handled smoothly to preserve a positive balance.

•)) **Gaining a commitment:** This is known as *'closing'* in sales jargon: an injunction to act does not cause people to agree, but it is often necessary to take the initiative and ask for their specific agreement, converting the interest you have generated into action.

The task here is multifaceted. The overall progress of the interaction must be controlled and managed, and at the same time individual techniques must be deployed as appropriate and how things are done adjusted in the light of how matters are progressing.

•)) **Follow up:** This is a simple description of a far-reaching activity. If agreement is made, then the contact may still need maintaining. If someone hesitates, then persistent chasing needs to take place, and yet doing so needs to be made acceptable. Beyond that, those with whom you have regular contact – as a manager does with their staff, or a member of staff does with their boss for that matter – will be influenced by the ongoing relationship. We are all more likely to co-operate with people with whom we have a good relationship, and to go along with what they say.

So the persuader needs to adopt a careful, systematic and creative approach, one demanding considerably more precision in the way it is done than the application of the traditional 'sales person's gift of the gab'. The key to it all is seeing things from the other person's point of view – the classic concept of empathy – and using that understanding to fine-tune approaches and ensure both persuasiveness and an approach that is acceptable to, and appeals to, those with whom you deal.

The right frame of mind

Make no mistake: the way you think about the process of persuasion is the first thing that conditions how well it goes and what results you will obtain. It is your attitude that decides how you will go about the detail of the task, and that in turn will influence how others see you and whether they will be willing to co-operate with you. You are, after all, usually the only person present on your side on the day. So, in part to illustrate the approaches that being persuasive demands, consider three key approaches you can take to what you do and how you do it, all of which can influence results positively.

Adopt the right overall approach

Let us start with an overall point and one that is of considerable significance. Any persuasive task must be regarded in the right way. Every circumstance and every person is different and everyone expects to be dealt with in a way that recognises just that.

What works best is, as a result, not any one set approach. You must deploy appropriate approaches from all the available techniques and do so person-by-person, meeting-by-meeting and day-by-day. The most persuasive people are those who recognise this fact. They seek to consciously fine-tune what they do; they never get stuck in a rut but always approach what they do intelligently and judge exactly how to proceed on each occasion in the light of all the circumstances.

This fact alone can be crucial. Because elements involved can be repetitive (for example, a committee Chairman may have to do similar things at every meeting), it is easy to find things starting to be done on 'automatic pilot' and that original and creative thinking about what is going on play a less important role.

Getting agreement rarely has very much to do with good luck. You can, however, to an extent, make your own luck; certainly you can and will do better if you see the process of working at it as a continuous one. This affects all the other points mentioned in this book. In other words, the person likely to be of most help to you in making your communications more effective is ultimately – yourself.

Be self-motivated

Every book, certainly every American book, about this sort of thing discusses the need for a positive mental attitude. No doubt this can help gain agreement, but you cannot pick positive mental attitudes off the trees or buy them in packs of six in the local supermarket. There are, however, certain factors that do assist self-motivation in a practical sense. The wise person uses these to boost their thinking and assist their performance. Here we consider two areas that work in this way: *confidence* and *persistence*.

First, let us consider *confidence*. This is a question of belief, and while it is perhaps impossible to show how to create this within yourself, certainly in a short paragraph, there is one overriding principle that helps. That is to use those tangible factors on which confidence rests. For example, if you have done your homework – you are prepared – this boosts confidence, giving you things you can be sure of which otherwise might be imponderables. Similarly, knowing your facts well, having clear objectives and arguments and what supports them being tried, tested and ready, all boost confidence. Bear this in mind as you read through this text and see how many of the topics reviewed can help build confidence in this way.

Second, consider *persistence*, a topic to which we return in a number of ways in the following pages. If you do more, rather than less, if you do more than others, then you know you are that much more likely to get your own way. By no means can everything be agreed in one quick fix; some things take time or need what is essentially a campaign before matters are tied down.

Develop the habit of reviewing everything you do, and answering one basic question: what can you do to make yourself more persuasive? And you might be surprised how much better you feel about what you can achieve.

Resolve to constantly fine-tune your approaches

There is an old saying that you can have five years' experience or just one year's experience repeated five times over. This is a simple yet vital principle. Experience needs to be taken and, at best, its accumulation accelerated. You should see every communications encounter you have as an opportunity to learn something that will help you make future ones work better, operating on the principle that even the best performance can be improved. The amount of information available from past encounters may be significant: the more you have persuasive encounters, the more you can equip yourself to do better in future ones. Constantly ask questions of yourself. Why did someone say that? Why did they voice that objection? Did they misunderstand something? Did they agree? What rang bells with them? If you can develop the habit of spending a moment replaying most of your encounters in your mind after you have finished them, then you can use this analysis to gradually evolve new approaches for the future. Fine-tune the way you work and avoid getting into a rut, repeating endlessly the same phrases as if they were a mantra as relevant to all the different people you see, and what you do is more likely to remain fresh and well directed each and every time.

But we are in danger of getting ahead of ourselves. We must concentrate on one persuasive encounter and think first about how you can act beforehand to influence its working well.

> **While the precise detail of what you do is crucial, everything that you do needs to reflect an appreciation of how decisions are made and how other individuals think and react. A focus on 'them rather than you' is another principle that must pervade everything you do – it is another catalyst to achieving what you want.**

CHAPTER 2

Preparing for Action

> *If you're not planning where you want to be,*
> *what excuse do you have for worrying about being*
> *nowhere?*
>
> **Tom Hopkins**
> **US management guru and author**

Although it was said earlier that there are no magic formulae, it is not exaggerating to suggest that preparation comes close. As an old saying has it: failing to plan is planning to fail. It need not take long, but it is always necessary – and it can make all the difference to the chances of success. It is effectively 'half the battle', and that is a good way to think about it. The person who runs rings around others is probably not inherently persuasive, but they are more likely to understand how this sort of communication works – and they 'do their homework'.

Essentially preparation does a number of things. It:

- •)) Clarifies the real purpose of what you want to do.

- •)) Provides a 'route map' to guide what you will do.

- •)) Helps you plan the 'shape' of the conversation/meeting.

- •)) Lets you decide the manner in which you will operate.

- •)) Allows you to anticipate and be ready for other people's responses (or as many of them as is possible).

- •)) Sets up your direction for the whole communication.

We will pick up all these points as we proceed. First, let us define preparation a little more. It ranges from just a few seconds' thought before you open your mouth, to a few minutes to get your mind straight about something in advance, to a longer session (including perhaps a discussion with someone else) to thrash out exactly how best to proceed. It may be helped by making some notes – either a few words on the back of an envelope or something more, depending on the complexity and import of what is being discussed.

Whatever is necessary, the first rule about preparation is very simple – always do it.

Whatever form your preparation takes, it needs to go through five stages. These are investigated in detail here, looking at the most that may be necessary. Simple situations can be approached with an abbreviated version of this thinking in mind (provided they *are* simpler). The stages are:

Setting objectives

This may sound complicated, or smack of over-engineering, but it is a way of clarifying your thinking. It is actually little more than being sure you can answer – clearly and precisely – the question *why* with regard to what you are to do. Many exchanges between people founder because one (or both) of them is not sure exactly what they are trying to do. Consider a simple example: you want your boss to increase your pay. This may sound straightforward (at least as an intention!) but, on examination, it is actually somewhat vague. Consider:

- •)) What exactly is 'pay'? (salary, benefits, annual bonus and what else?)

- •)) By how much do you want it increased? (An extra day's pay is an increase, so is 10% more or 50% more?)

- •)) When do you want this to happen? (today, in a month's time, next year?)

- •)) Many details, these and more, remain unspecified in the base description *I want to get a pay rise.*

A much-quoted acronym says that objectives should be SMART. That is, objectives should be:

- ·))) Specific.

- ·))) Measurable.

- ·))) Achievable.

- ·))) Realistic.

- ·))) Timed.

Examining how this relates to the chosen example of a pay rise, and the simplest description of it, *I want my boss to increase my pay*, illustrates how viewing objectives this way helps us have a really clear purpose in mind. Thus:

- ·))) **Is it specific?** Not very – you may need to put a number, or at least a range of numbers, to it before it qualifies as a genuine objective in this sense.

- ·))) **Is it measurable?** Not really – practically anything qualifies as an increase. If we put a firm figure to it – 10%, say, translated into an actual figure – then it can be measured accurately. Afterwards you will know for sure whether you have obtained it or not.

- ·))) **Is it achievable?** Well, that depends on how it is actually defined. If you decide to go for say a 50% increase that might definitely not be achievable – you have to pick a figure that relates not only to what you would like, but also to what is likely to be possible.

- ·))) **Is it realistic?** This means not 'can I get this?' (is it achievable?), but asks the question 'should I?'. It is influenced by questions such as: How will your request be seen? Will it be viewed as being reasonable? Will it mark you down as a troublemaker, or a mouse? Taking this broader view is also an important part of setting appropriate objectives.

•))) **What timing?** This too needs to be specific, and be so in two ways: first, what do you want to achieve at a particular meeting or at the end of next week? And second, when do you want action to be taken? – say, aiming for next month's salary slip to reflect an increased figure?

This kind of thinking simply acts to formalise what you want to achieve. It is very difficult to decide how exactly to proceed if your intentions are vague. Remember the old saying: if you don't know where you are going, any road will do. Clearly stated intentions are directional: that is, they link logically to conducting a well-planned meeting or exchange; one that is more likely to work for you and get you your own way.

Checking the facts

Some degree of research may be useful at this stage. Research might only be a formal word for what may only be a little routine checking. If you are trying to persuade someone you have never met of something or you are dealing with something complex, then research may be the best word. You may need to find out something about them: what they do, whom they work for, what and whom they know and how they may think about things. This may mean talking to other people. In a work situation it might indicate some external research. This might mean checking company directories, a website or an annual report to find out something about any organisation for which someone works. As we will see, a few additional facts may be very useful. And making assumptions instead of using facts can be very dangerous; linking what you say to something that is not true of the other person is unlikely to ring bells.

Returning to the salary increase example, a series of simple checks – when you last had an increase, what percentage it was, what trends are current in your industry, what national cost of living figures show and so on – may take only a few moments and yet prove disproportionately useful. A meeting might stall almost instantly on a question you are unable to answer: *What's the national figure for pay increases been in the last year?*

Think here about what information you *definitely* need to have at your fingertips, and what you *might* need. Doing just a little more thinking and checking in this way than the bare minimum may prove a great asset as communication gets underway.

Planning the meeting

Whatever exchange is envisaged, and it may be your contribution to a meeting, a one-to-one discussion across a desk or a brief conversation 'on the stairs', you need to have some idea of how *ideally* you would like it to go. This means thinking about the structure. What will be best for you to say first, second and third? How will you state your case? What examples or evidence do you need? How are the points you make likely to be received? And so on.

The fact that you know that no meeting will go exactly as you plan – simply because people are unpredictable – should not stop this thinking from being done. The task will be to get things to go *as closely as possible* to your ideal, and to be able to cope with any divergences along the way as well in a way that keeps your case as closely as possible to the way you consider ideal. The figure on page 36 shows this concept graphically.

The objectives you have set will influence your decisions here. For example, if the salary increase you want is unashamedly high, then more may need to be done to get the boss to listen and take your request seriously, and more evidence may be necessary to support that case.

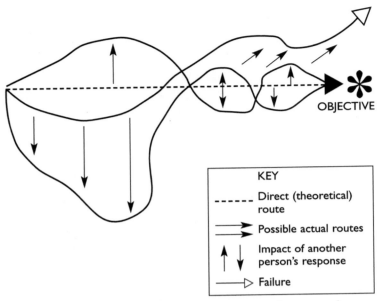

KEY

- - - - - Direct (theoretical) route

———▶ Possible actual routes

↑ ↓ Impact of another person's response

———▷ Failure

Figure 2: Structuring and directing a conversation towards your objective

Backing up what you will say

Though you intend your argument to be powerful, just stating it may not be enough to get what you want agreed. This part of the planning process is concerned with what can support your case and how it can be organised.

Seeing is believing. Think how much more difficult it is to refuse a dessert in a restaurant when there is a trolley of the actual desserts wheeled unasked to your elbow. Similarly you need to think about what you might show someone: a picture, a graph, detailed figures, or an 'exhibit' (as when your decision about which new curtains to buy is influenced by the swatch you take home to look at in your own living room). The range of possibilities here is enormous. You should ask yourself what things would be useful, rather than just what happens to be available, as it may be worth some effort to create something to show.

Whatever you decide to incorporate into the making of your case, make sure it is well organised. It can be impressive to produce something right on cue, perhaps from a mass of material, and it can make a greater impression if it is introduced as being specially for the other person – *I thought this might make it easier for you to imagine.*

Note too that one of the things that may, in more complex situations, add to your case is another person; two or more of you working as a team. Selecting who it should be, and sorting out who will lead, who will do what and organising so that you work together seamlessly needs care. Well done, two (or more) people operating effectively together can add to the positive nature of the impression given. Conversely, lack of co-ordination may give a disproportionate negative impression – of lack of organisation, of lack of care, concern or competence and do no good at all.

Focus on the feelings of others

Preparation, reviewed more specifically earlier in this chapter, may not be a magic formula that guarantees success, but it will certainly help. So too does the factor described next. The premise is absurdly simple: you are more likely to be persuasive if you approach the process as something that relates as much to what *other people* want and how they think, as to what you want to do yourself (hence the *helping people decide* definition set out earlier). Indeed, this perspective must underlie everything you do, so the starting point is to think through how being persuaded, and perhaps going along with it too, looks from the other person's point of view.

In addition to the specific thinking process of how people go about making a decision to agree to act, or not, there are two further aspects to other people's views that need to be considered and then borne in mind as you plan to communicate with them:

- •)) How they feel.

- •)) What they want.

Other people's feelings

Most often people recognise very quickly when they are in a situation where someone is trying to persuade them about something. Their instinctive reaction may be to dislike the idea of it – *I'm not being made to do anything*, they say to themselves. However, once they begin to appreciate what is being asked of them, their actual feelings may be positive or negative, or indeed a mixture of both. Positive reactions are clearly easier to deal with, and can work for us to make achieving success easier.

In an obvious case – persuading someone to do something they will clearly find beneficial – they may start to see it as a good idea almost at once. So, say to someone that you want to discuss some changes to their work portfolio that will make their life easier and put them in line for a salary increase, and they will be all ears. This does not mean that they will not be on the lookout in case what is being suggested is not one hundred per cent good, but essentially their thinking will tend to be positive. In this case, there may well be no difficult implications for the person doing the persuading, other than to aim to build on the goodwill that is already starting to exist.

But the opposite may, perhaps more often, be the case. A variety of negative feelings may arise, immediately or as you get into making your case, and if so then you need to be sensitive to what is happening and seek to position what you do in light of it. For instance, if the change referred to in the last paragraph is stated baldly and devoid of any context or explanation – *There must be some changes* – it will almost certainly prompt objections.

The following sets out some typical examples of how people might feel and what they might think. They might feel:

- •))) **Insecure:** Thinking – this sounds complicated, I am not sure I will know how to decide or what view to take.

- •))) **Threatened:** Thinking – things are being taken out of my hands, *I* should decide this, not be pushed into something by someone else.

•))) **Out of control:** Thinking – if I make the wrong decision I may be in trouble, any decision involves taking a risk and things could backfire on me.

•))) **Worried:** Thinking – you are suggesting changes – does that imply I was wrong or at fault before? I don't like that implication.

•))) **Exposed:** Thinking – this discussion is getting awkward, I am being asked to reveal facts or feelings that I would rather not discuss.

•))) **Ignorant:** Thinking – you are using your greater knowledge to put me on the spot, I don't feel confident in arguing the point though I am not convinced.

•))) **Confused:** Thinking – I know I ought to understand, but you are not making things clear – or letting me get any clarification.

•))) **Sceptical:** Thinking – you make it sound good, but then it is what *you* want, maybe the case is not as strong as it seems.

•))) **Misunderstood:** Thinking – I don't believe the case you make takes my point of view into account – it's all right for you, but not for me.

•))) **Suspicious:** Thinking – people with 'something to sell' always exaggerate and are only interested in what they want – I am not going to be caught out by this.

Who both parties are, and their relationship, clearly affects things here. For instance, someone may have more reservations as they recognise they are about to be persuaded by someone with more age, experience or authority than they have. But a moment's thought quickly suggests all such feelings (and you may add more) are understandable, but if they are overlooked, if you go ahead as if your message should be received with open arms when in fact such reactions exist – you will surely hit problems. If thoughts such as this *are* in people's minds, then they can act to cloud the issue and may make it more difficult for them to see the, perhaps genuine, logic of something you are suggesting. It is not enough to be clear or to present what seems to you an obviously strong case – the other person must see it as something with which they can willingly go along. Thus if you recognise that such feelings exist, then you must allow for them in the way you plan and execute what you do.

What others want

What people want may vary enormously, of course. It will relate back to their situation, views, experience and prejudices. It may reflect deep-seated, long-held views or be more topical and transient – or both. Sometimes you know in advance what people want. On other occasions it comes out in the course of conversation, or you need to ferret it out as you go along. It can be complicated – with a number of different 'wants' involved together (some of which could well be contradictory) – and thus needs some thought to keep it in mind. But understanding and responding to people's desires is an important part of being persuasive.

A simple example will make what is involved here clearer. Imagine you have to make some sort of formal presentation jointly with a colleague; this might be at work or in a situation like being a member of a committee. You want to persuade them to set aside sufficient time – in advance – to rehearse the presentation together to make sure it goes well. What might they want in this situation? Maybe to:

- •)) **Make sure it goes well:** As you do, but maybe they are more confident of making it go well than you are.

- •)) **Minimise time spent in preparation:** Like you again no doubt, but perhaps their being busy blinds them to the need for rehearsal, which they might see as being a sledgehammer to crack a nut.

- •)) **Leave preparation to the last minute:** Perhaps because other tasks have, for them, greater short-term urgency, or seem to have.

•))) **Outshine you on the day:** They might be more intent on scoring personal points with someone, than on making sure that the overall event goes well.

These are examples only; many feelings might be involved depending on the nature of the presentation, how important it is and how someone feels about it. One thing is clear, however: such wants make a difference to the likelihood of your getting agreement. Even in a simple example like this the individual viewpoints are clear: 1) you both want it to go well, but take differing views of what is necessary to make this happen. 2) in general you want the same thing, but would define the amount of time that constitutes the minimum needed to prepare differently. 3) here you differ, and on 4) there are very personal wants that are, to a degree, outside of the main objective involved that of making your individual presentations work seamlessly together.

There is a need to balance the differing viewpoints if agreement is to be forthcoming. If you are the persuader, you feel your viewpoint is right – or at least that it is the most appropriate option (there is rarely ever only one way to approach anything that can be definitively described as 'right'). How do you move them towards your view? Clearly, doing so involves them adjusting their intentions. You do not have to persuade them to change their views completely. For instance, they may always see it as easier to do whatever preparation is involved at the last minute, but they may still agree to set a time when you want or – compromise may often be involved – somewhere between your two views.

Thinking through this sort of thing so that you have such considerations clearly in mind is always useful.

How decisions are made

Remember how the process of persuasion was defined in terms of *helping people*. Thus, whatever the commitment is that you are looking to secure, the process of obtaining it is best viewed as one that assists people to make a decision – and which, at the same time, encourages them to make it in favour of whatever option you are suggesting. In a purchasing situation the choices involve competition: if you are buying a washing machine, say, then you may find yourself having to decide whether to purchase the Hoover, the Indesit, the Bosch or whatever (as well as decide where to buy it from and what to pay). In other situations choice is still involved. In the presentation example used earlier, your imagined colleague will decide between rehearsing or not, rehearsing earlier or later, doing so in a way that helps them or both of you and so on. Doing nothing may seem, in many circumstances, an attractive option and sometimes needs as much arguing against as any other.

It follows that, if a process of decision making is inherently involved, you should not fight against it. The intention should be to encourage and *help* it to take place. Persuasive communication is not something you direct at other people. It is something you *engage in with them*. The difference is crucial, and anything that leads you to see it as a one-way process is likely to end up making the tasks you seek to accomplish more difficult. So far so good, but how exactly do people make decisions?

This was defined earlier and the answer can be summed up succinctly. People:

- •)) Consider the options.

- •)) Consider the advantages and disadvantages of each.

- •)) *Weigh up* the overall way in which they compare.

- •)) Select what seems to be, on balance, the best course of action to take.

This does not mean finding and selecting an option with no downsides; realistically this may simply not be possible. It means assessing things and selecting an acceptable option, one where the pluses outweigh the minuses. The analogy suggested of a balance or weighing scales is a good one to keep in mind. Imagine an old-fashioned weighing scales with a container on each side. One contains a variety of plus signs, the other minuses. The signs are of different sizes because some elements of the argument are more important than others are – they weigh more heavily on the scales. Additionally, some signs represent tangible matters. Others are more subjective – just as, in the presentation example above, achieving the right results from undertaking it (say getting agreement to a 10% increase on a budget) is something tangible. Whereas an individual's desire to increase their status within an organisation through the way they are perceived as a presenter is intangible. Intangible some points may be, but they can still be a powerful component of any case. It is these sorts of factors that must pervade your thinking as you prepare, if that preparation is to be worthwhile.

A final point completes the picture here: some decisions are more important than others and therefore may be seen to warrant more thought. Where a decision is of this sort, people may actively want it to be *well considered*. They want to feel that the process of making it has been sensible and thorough (and therefore the decision is more likely to be a good one); and they may want other people (their manager, say) to feel the same. In either case, this feeling may lengthen the process of persuading them.

With this preparatory thinking done, you are ready to communicate. Before you start you should know:

- •)) Precisely what you are aiming at (note: here it might be useful to think of a personal example of something you need to do to keep in mind as you read on).

- •)) How you intend to go about presenting your case.

- •)) Something about the other person – and therefore their likely reactions.

- •)) What you will use to exemplify your case (and have such things organised and ready for use).

- •)) What problems may occur and, broadly, how you will deal with them.

It may also be important to think about certain other matters. For example, how much time are you likely to have to make your case? It is no good planning a blindingly convincing case that takes half an hour to deliver, if you realistically will only have half that time. Consider too: where will you be? Will there be room for you to lay all the materials you plan to use out on the table? *Note:* if you have to deal with people on other than a face-to-face basis, remember that other techniques may be involved, for example writing a proposal or an 'on-your-feet' presentation*, and that this can add an additional dimension to the preparation process that also needs some thought.

You can never know, of course, exactly how things will go and your planning must not act as a straightjacket, but must allow you to retain an inherent flexibility. Yet having all this clear in your mind will certainly help; what is more, it adds another important element to the equation – and to your chances of getting your own way. What is that? It is the confidence factor, already mentioned. If you are clear in your own mind of the path ahead, and have to make less of it up as you go along, then what you do will always be easier – and make a positive result more likely.

We will return to some of the issues highlighted here in subsequent chapters, particularly those that follow the sequence of events when you meet with someone. The next chapter looks at how you get off to a good start as you enter that sequence.

FOOTNOTE: * I have written about presentations in *How to craft successful business presentations and effective public speaking* – another Foulsham title that may be useful to you.

Preparation is a key preliminary to success. The way in which you approach it, and how you go about it, can put you in a position to conduct the best conversation that will persuade someone to go along with what you want. Always do it.

CHAPTER 3

First Impressions Last

*I am the world's worst salesman, therefore I must
make it easy for people to buy.*

F W Woolworth
Head of the retail chain

What you do and how you do it matters: all of it. So from the very
first moment, the way you go about things will affect the likelihood
of success. Perhaps even before you open your mouth, and certainly
before you have said any great amount, people will make judgements
based on how you communicate.

Your communication style no doubt reflects your personality.
Certainly there is no intention here to suggest that you forget or
disguise that and adopt some contrived manner in the belief that this
will make you more persuasive; it will not. More likely a forced style
will seem just that and may well act to make you less effective.

On the other hand you do need to think about how you come over.
Will it help your case to be seen in any particular way? For instance to
be seen as: knowledgeable, expert, caring, friendly, responsive,
adaptable, secure, well organised, efficient, forward thinking,
confident, interested (particularly in the other person or the topic
under discussion), respectful, consistent, reliable or whatever? (and
what do you *not* want to appear?). Is it important that you display an
attention to detail, a respect for the other person's time or that you
'look the part' in some way? Many factors might be involved and such
a list could doubtless be extended.

The point is not only that there are many such factors that can be
listed, but also that they are *all options*. You can *elect* to come over as,
say, confident or expert (to some degree even if you are not!). You can

46

emphasise factors that are important to the other person; indeed, you need to anticipate what these will be. If they want to dot every i and cross every t, so be it; you need to become the sort of person who does just that if it will allow you to get your own way in the end.

This is not so contrived, just an exaggerated version of what we do all the time as we communicate with different kinds of people – for example at opposite ends of the organisational hierarchy. Again a little thought ahead of actually communicating can allow you to pitch things in the right kind of way, so that your manner enhances the chances of getting your own way – rather than negates it.

Two factors are especially important here:

- •)) **Projection:** This word is used to encapsulate your approach, personality, authority, clout and the whole way in which you come over.

- •)) **Empathy:** This is the ability to see things from other people's point of view. More than that, it is the ability to *be seen* to see things from other people's point of view.

These act together. Too much projection and you come over as dictatorial and aggressive. Too little empathy and you seem insensitive and uncaring. You need to deploy both, and they go well together. Sufficient empathy softens what might otherwise be seen as a too powerful approach, and makes the net effect acceptable. The figure on page 48 illustrates how this can help focus your approach.

This may only necessitate a few words being changed, with an unacceptable – *I think you should do this* – being replaced by something like – *Given that you feel timing is so important, you may want to do this.*

At this point, well prepared and with a close eye on how the other person will consider your suggestion, and in what way they will go about coming to a decision to go along with it or not, we can turn to how to structure and put over a persuasive case and, for the moment, how to make an effective start.

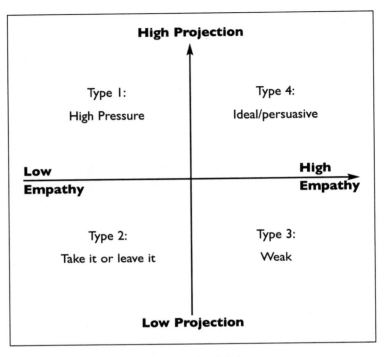

Figure 3: 'Different strokes for different folks'

Your communication may take various forms, but from now on let us concentrate particularly on the ubiquitous meeting. This may be formal, with two people (or more) sitting comfortably around a desk or kitchen table, or happen on the move (walking from the office to the pub for lunch); and sometimes it will occur in more difficult circumstances (like a discussion, on your feet, in a factory with noisy machinery clattering in the background). In every case the objective is the same: to create a considered message that acts persuasively to prompt someone to take whatever action you seek.

In order to be able to proceed on a considered basis, you need to draw on a clear view of what is happening during such a meeting. We will dissect the process to tease out the key issues, and focus now on the first moments.

A good start

The manner you adopt, and the preparation you have done, will both contribute to your making a good start. So too will your attitude at the beginning. You need to take charge. View it as your meeting. Make it one that you will direct. This need not imply an aggressive stance. Just as a good Chairperson may not speak first, loudest or longest, you can effectively put yourself in the driving seat without making the other person feel overpowered. So, take the initiative and aim to *run* the kind of meeting you want – and that the other person will find appropriate and will like.

The first task is to get their attention, and to make them concentrate on the issue at hand. You will never persuade anybody of anything if they are not concentrating on, and thus appreciating, what is involved. Imagine what they are thinking – *is this going to be interesting, useful or a waste of good time?* – and aim to make sure that their first reaction is as you would want it. Perhaps something like – *this seems as if it will be useful. So far so good. Let's see what they have to say.*

To create this impression it helps if you:

- •)) Appear well organised and prepared.

- •)) Suggest and agree an agenda that makes sense to you both.

- •)) Make clear how long the session will (probably) last.

- •)) Get down to business promptly.

Overall, if in the first moments you show interest in the other person and make it clear that they are important to the proceedings, this will certainly help. Even something as simple as a little flattery may help – *Some of your good organisation would help here, John. Can you spare ten minutes to go through …* Of course, not everyone is susceptible to this sort of thing …… hold on a moment, if you just said *That's right* to yourself, you have shown how useful this method can be!

A final point here about getting hold of the meeting is worth mentioning, although it is relevant primarily at the more formal end of things. This is the simple expedient of setting an agenda. Let me be more specific: of suggesting the agenda you want and which you feel will make being persuasive easiest, yet making the other person feel this is useful. First think through how you feel something is best dealt with, have it clear in your mind (and put it in writing for the more formal meetings). Then table it assumptively: *It may well be helpful to have an agenda in mind, not least so that we can do this in a reasonable time. Perhaps I could suggest ...* In other words, put it over as something the both of you will find useful. Even if it is only three items – *Let's take X first and then talk about Y and Z* – this is a powerful technique. You may, especially with a longer list, prompt counter-suggestions and have to compromise a little, but simply taking the initiative means that suggestions are often agreed wholesale.

The result is that you can then take things in the order you want. Furthermore, once the agenda is agreed, you can introduce things progressively – not as what you want, but rather as what they want (or at least agreed to). Thus, say: *What we agreed to take next was ...* rather than something that starts with the word I.

Incidentally, it is worth noting as it goes with the agenda, the duration of a meeting is best put out in the open, even if it is an estimate. If you tell people what they are likely to be in for – *Let's take half an hour or so to ...* – they like it and can then mentally position where you are in the total process at any particular moment. If people just do not know whether something might take a few minutes or all day, it is unsettling, not least to their concentration on what you are saying.

Finding out

With the meeting under way, the next stage is to find out something about the other person's perspective on the matter before you move straight into telling them what you want. This may well build on knowledge you already have of course (especially if you know the person concerned), and in simple situations may only link to a few key facts, but in more complex situations it may take up some time and unearth a considerable amount of useful information. For example, returning to the example of a presentation rehearsal, it may be useful to know whether your colleague:

•))) Wants to rehearse.

•))) Needs to do so.

•))) Sees it being done at any particular moment.

•))) Envisages it taking a particular amount of time.

Importantly it is also likely to help to know what they believe the presentation should achieve and how exactly it might be done, and so on. Having some knowledge of this kind of thinking, and perhaps of their presentational abilities, shows you something about the job of persuasion to be done. This may range from a major battle (they do not want to do it at all), to a near meeting of minds (you both see the need, but you are going to have to persuade them to give up a longer amount of time for it than they first envisaged).

Such finding out is achieved by asking questions – and, of course, by *listening* to the answers. Each is worth a comment.

Questioning

What to ask and how to put it may need some thought as you prepare. You need to phrase questions clearly and it is useful to use three levels of questioning.

•))) **Closed questions:** These prompt rapid *Yes* or *No* answers, and are useful as a starting point or to gain rapid confirmation of something.

•)) **Open questions:** These *cannot* be answered *Yes* or *No* and typically begin with the words what, why, where, when, who and how and phrases like *Tell me about* .... They get people talking, they involve them and they like the feeling they give to the conversation.

•)) **Probing questions:** These are simply a series of linked questions to pursue a point – *Tell me more about* ..., particularly to get to the why of the matter.

An example from the business world appears in the boxed paragraph below. The principle may help with any situation, however. To extend the presentation example: ask your colleague if there should be a presentation rehearsal and the yes or no answer tells you little. Follow up a yes answer by asking why they think it is necessary (an open question) and you will learn more – *I'm really a bit nervous about the whole thing* – and more questions can then fill in the detail.

Information to assist persuasion: questioning techniques

Let us illustrate the sequence of questioning possible and what it can do by quoting a possible conversation between a travel agent and one of his prospects (a business manager involved in export).

Agent: *'What areas are currently your priority, Mr Export Manager?'*

Prospect: 'The Middle East is top priority for investigation but, short term, Germany has been more important.'

Agent: *'What makes that so?'*

Prospect: 'Well, we're exhibiting at a trade fair in Germany. This will tie up a number of staff and eat up a lot of the budget. Our exploratory visit to the Middle East may have to wait.'

Agent: *'Won't that cause problems, seeing as you had intended to go earlier?'*

Prospect: 'I suppose it will. With the lead times involved, it may rule out the chances of tying up any deals for this financial year.'

Agent: *'Had you thought of moving one of your people straight on from Germany to the Middle East, Mr Export Manager?'*

Prospect: 'Err, no.'

Agent: *'I think I could show some real savings over making two separate trips. If you did it this way, the lead time might not slip. Would that be of interest?'*

Prospect: 'Could be. If I give you some dates, can you map something out to show exactly how it could be done?'

Agent: *'Certainly . . .'*

This kind of questioning not only produces information, but can also be used creatively to spot opportunities. Here it accurately pinpoints the prospect's real needs and allows a precise response to them. Most people not only like talking about their own situation but react favourably to this approach. They may well see the genuine identification of their problems and the offer of solutions to them as distinctly different to any competitive approach they have received that simply catalogues the product or services offered.

In this case, it also allows much better demonstration of two factors that purchasers look for from travel agents: objectivity and expertise. The more this aspect of the case they make predominates, the more the travel agency is differentiated from any potential competition. And the more likely he or she is to get their business.

It is important here that people appreciate what is happening. Clever questioning may provide you with a useful picture, but this needs to be seen to be the case. You will persuade more certainly if the other person knows that you understand their position.

More information

Two further points are worth noting here, both linked to the earlier comment that people need to know that you understand. You can usefully use the following techniques.

- •)) **Agree the information:** Using a phraseology that makes it clear that you understand is more powerful, and affects the later conversation more than just a simple acknowledgement such as *Right*. So say something about a point: *You mention the importance of timing. This is certainly something we must consider. Do you … ?*, linking it into further questions if necessary and making the point that you have taken it on board. You can use this later as you lead into a topic, saying something like, *Earlier you said that timing was important. One of the factors here is …* This makes what you have to say on the matter more like a response to them, than a point you wish to push. The psychology here is important.

- •)) **Check the priority:** Often people make undifferentiated statements. For example: *I suppose I'm looking for something interesting, worthwhile but which does not take up too much time.* This is something that might be said by someone considering serving on a committee. All true no doubt, but what is most important? For example, the need to do something interesting and worthwhile might outweigh the time consideration. In other words, a stated maximum time involvement might be breached if other things particularly appealed. Just asking, *You mention several things. What actually is most important?* can give you additional and useful information.

Listen to what people say

It is very easy to fail to listen as carefully as you should. Imagine someone says to you, 'The sky is bright green today, so ...'. You disagree. Manifestly it is blue. What is your mind doing? Not listening carefully to what comes next, but planning a riposte. Watch for others doing this to you; it is a classic cause of misunderstandings. There are all sorts of reasons why listeners might drift off – if you are aware how easy it is for it to happen, it is the first step to preventing it.

The moral is to listen carefully. Listening is important in any persuasive conversation; indeed, throughout it. But this is reviewed at this point as it is clearly especially vital when questioning is taking place. You will look at least careless, and at worst incompetent or rude, if you say something later on that makes it clear that you have not been listening properly to what someone has said to you. Listening is actually easier said than done; there may be many distractions and your mind is necessarily on a number of things at once: what to say next, what to ask and so on. There is an old saying that mankind was made with two ears and one mouth and that that is the right proportion in which to use them, so you must listen carefully and that means what is called *active* listening. Some ideas about this follow, in checklist style:

Active listening to obtain information

1. **Want to listen:** This is easy once you realise how much doing so can help in being persuasive.

2. **Look like a good listener:** If they can see they have your attention, people will be more forthcoming.

3. **Understand:** It is not just the words but what lies behind them that you must note.

4. **React:** Let them see you have heard, understood and are interested. Nods, small comments and so on will encourage the flow of information and response you are getting.

5. **Stop talking:** Other than small comments, you cannot listen and talk simultaneously. Do not interrupt.

6. **Use empathy:** Put yourself in the other person's shoes and make sure you really appreciate their point of view.

7. **Check:** If necessary, ask questions to clarify matters as the conversation proceeds. An understanding based, even partly, on guesses is dangerous. But ask diplomatically: do not say, *You did not explain that very well.*

8. **Remain unemotional:** Too much thinking ahead – *However will I cope with that objection?* – can distract.

9. **Concentrate:** Allow nothing to distract you.

10. **Look at people:** Be sure to engage people, give them your attention and maintain eye contact; anything less can easily be read as nervousness, disinterest or worse.

11. **Note particularly the key points:** Edit what is said in your mind to make what you need to retain manageable.

12. **Avoid personalities:** It is the ideas and information that matter, not what you think of the person; this can distract.

13. **Do not lose yourself in subsequent argument:** Some thinking ahead may be necessary (you can actually listen faster than people can talk, so this is possible); indulge in too much thinking rather than listening and you risk suddenly finding that you have missed something.

14. **Avoid negatives:** To begin with at least, signs of disagreement, even a visual one, can make people clam up.

15. **Make notes:** Do not trust your memory. If it is polite to do so, and the matter has sufficient complexity, ask permission to make notes.

Adhering to this checklist will help you listen more and miss less; and both can make a difference.

Make no mistake. Finding out can give you information that becomes the basis of successful persuasion. If your fellow presenter lets slip that their boss has said this 'better go well', then later you might use that as part of your argument – *given what your boss said about it, perhaps the time we spend beforehand could be a little longer.* Any conversation can produce opportunities to do this if you really listen; as in LISTEN. Besides, people love to be listened to, so it all helps create the right feeling for the conversation.

Different strokes for different folks

It is said that there are two kinds of people in the world: those that divide people into categories, and the rest. More seriously, while everyone is an individual and must be treated as such, there are types of people who do differ in their response to a persuasive case. Sorting such categories in the mind is perhaps a good start to being able to deal in the right kind of way with all the different types of people you meet. It provides a manageable basis for dealing with the decisions involved. The following is not intended to be definitive, you may well come across people who do not quite fit in any of the following categories, but it provides a basis for planning and deciding how to deal with people and maybe for devising additional categories of your own.

Certainly, it is possible to categorise people, at least in a general sense and in a way that helps you to get off on the right foot with them, and makes it more likely that they will respond positively. The sort of way this is usually represented is shown in the figure on page 58 contrasting just two differing factors on two axes reflecting people's differing attitudes.

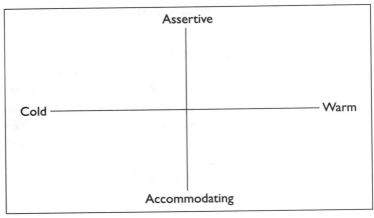

Figure 4: Types of person

Four main types are significant, and they are sufficiently different to demand different approaches. This is perhaps best described with reference to their likely differing attitudes to persuasion, stated below as they might describe them.

Type 1: assertive / cold

People with 'something to sell' cannot be trusted. They are determined to push me into something that I neither want nor need. I must therefore be tough and resistant. The best defence against such people is offence.

Type 2: accommodating / cold

Such people cannot be trusted. To defend myself I try to avoid them and, if I can't, I stay as uninvolved and unresponsive as possible.

Type 3: accommodating / warm

It's people who matter most. If I like someone and believe that they like me, then I will listen and tend to believe what they say.

Type 4: assertive / warm

I like to make my own decisions and do so on a well-considered basis. I go along most readily with people who show that they understand me and demonstrate that they have a case that makes sense to me.

With this in mind, it is possible to think about what approach makes it most likely to create a rapport with such people, especially early on and if you do not know them well.

How to deal with Type I: assertive / cold people

- •)) Do not expect a warm welcome.

- •)) Accept their negative attitude, and use your professionalism as a foil.

- •)) Keep small talk to an absolute minimum.

- •)) Emphasise that you are there for sound reasons.

- •)) Make your opening remarks short and very much to the point.

- •)) Do not be intimidated.

- •)) Do not try to be clever by using what these people will consider 'pushy ploys'.

- •)) Appear to let them take the lead, but demonstrate your *control* of the interview by attentive listening, note-taking if necessary, and asking concise, factual and open questions, which will, in fact, help direct the meeting.

- •)) Be firm and polite but never appear subservient.

- •)) Position yourself as confident, professional and calmly determined.

How to deal with Type 2: accommodating / cold people

•)) Expect these people to appear cool and distant, and understand that you will be seen as a threat to their security until you have won their trust.

•)) Be calm, professional and unhurried.

•)) Avoid pressure tactics.

•)) Do not say too much during the opening moments of a conversation. Let them 'size you up' for themselves, and do not cloud their picture of you by being flashy, brash or pushy.

•)) Some small talk is recommended.

•)) Do not expect to get agreement instantly from these people (it may take time and several conversations).

•)) If possible, position yourself as an advisor.

How to deal with Type 3: accommodating / warm people

•)) Expect a warm welcome, but understand that these people welcome everyone: their warmth does not necessarily mean you are particularly special.

•)) Allow them to express their feelings with some small talk, but stay in control and do not let them lose sight of the fact that you are there for serious reasons.

•)) As these people like to feel they belong to select groups, mention as early as possible something about your standing and why the discussion is appropriate.

•)) Tell them exactly how you would like to structure the conversation, including your role and theirs.

•))) Do not appear too officious or clinical by rushing the pace, or by taking too many notes: keep the opening conversational.

•))) Position yourself as someone they 'would like to do business with'.

How to deal with Type 4: assertive / warm people

•))) Expect a correct and professional greeting (and probably a firm handshake).

•))) Take your time to get organised in a way that seems businesslike.

•))) Demonstrate your own professionalism, and understand that these people will expect your acknowledgement of their position or importance.

•))) Your opening remarks must be natural (not contrived), short and clearly indicate that you already know a fair amount about them and their circumstances (even if initially only in a general sense).

•))) Do not be dogmatic: they will want you to be flexible so that their ideas and objectives can be accommodated in a *joint* solution.

•))) Be prepared to revise your planned objectives.

•))) Avoid a fixed or rigid 'stock' approach.

•))) Position yourself as a creative, experienced operator.

Respect of the people's individuality, taking an accurate view of what 'type' of person you are dealing with and making a real attempt to 'get on their wavelength' early on in the proceedings will always help you in any encounter. Persuasive technique is not, after all, something to be applied slavishly or by rote, but something to be deployed intelligently case by case. And the variable that dictates exactly how that deployment should vary is the other person. Everyone is different, and it is a dangerous mistake to treat them as if they were all alike.

Overall, the first stage dealt with in this chapter will not last that long, but at the end of it you should feel things are well under way. The other person should be feeling that what you are saying is interesting and they should want to hear more. You should also be well on the way to establishing any authority you need and be able to move ahead on the basis of a reasonable and accurate view of how the other person is feeling and thinking.

Next, with that done you can begin the main task, that of putting over your case.

To say you only get one chance to make a good first impression may be a cliché, but it is true. Time and effort spent getting off to a good start always pays dividends: the good start builds your confidence and ensures others want to follow what you say. In addition, if you find out about people, what you can do will always be more personalised and more appreciated; and if you find out more than someone else offering the same person an alternative, then everything else you do will be easier for you and more difficult for them.

CHAPTER 4

The Persuasive Core of the Communication

There is no such thing as a minor detail. All details are major.

Anon

This is the heartland of the whole process: *the persuasive core of every meeting.*

Whatever else needs to be done, and whatever else may exert influence over the degree of impact you have, there is a major job to be done here. It is here that you must be most specifically persuasive, yet there is more to it than that. Whatever you must do to put across your case (this can include description, illustration and perhaps even demonstration) must be done carefully and in a way that increases the power of the picture you are building up in people's minds. You must also differentiate, as it is here that people are not only weighing up what you say, they are making their most direct comparisons with any other options that they may be considering in parallel. In many contexts it is sensible to assume there *are* other options incidentally, and never assume they are anything but compelling; even asking for a pay rise may prompt a manager to think what else they might spend that money on or who might deserve it more. The factors reviewed in this chapter are all directed at increasing the effectiveness of what you do in this central area of the persuasion process.

What it means to be persuasive

Remember that people want to make decisions *their* way. They want to think about whatever proposition you are making to them; they want to assess it and make what they would regard as a considered decision.

An effective approach must take this thinking process (described earlier) into account and match the thinking – so that what you do really is seen as helping people to weigh things up, but it must also be persuasive; your approach must work for you as well as fit with the thinking of others. So what do we mean by 'persuasive'?

My dictionary says of the word persuasion: to cause (a person) to believe or do something by reasoning with them. Fine, but the question is *how* to do this. To be persuasive a case must exhibit three key characteristics. Thus we can define 'persuasive' as a communications approach that is seen as being:

- •)) Understandable.

- •)) Attractive.

- •)) Convincing.

None of these on their own is enough to secure agreement, and together they must not only make a strong case, they may also need to differentiate your case from competition and do so powerfully enough to make you and what you suggest first choice. As we have seen, persuasion must be based on others' feelings and situations, and identifying these is a priority. Using this knowledge is a priority too. There is no point in asking someone a number of questions and then manifestly not taking their situation into account as you go on to explain in detail what you want them to do.

Perhaps the first rule here is that your approach must be individually tailored to give each and every person what they want, an approach which they see respects their point of view, which matches their situation and so generates more immediate interest. Differences are quickly apparent if, for instance, you think about communication up, down and around an organisation – everyone is different.

Bearing this in mind will get you off on the right track and will quickly show the reason why a degree of preparation added to by obtaining the answers to some well-directed questions are both so important. But this is a complex stage; there are many disparate things to be done; yet the whole stage must proceed smoothly. This is important to your personal positioning: if it is handled smoothly, if it appears well thought out and relevant (because it is!), then anyone you are dealing with will conclude they are dealing with a 'professional' and take more serious note of what you say.

Now, we consider in turn the three key criteria that, together, create persuasiveness and how you can put them to work.

Make what you say understandable

It is probable that more cases fail to convince because of lack of (easy) understanding than for any other more complex reason. This is certainly true if the topic under discussion is of any complexity. And the reason (first touched on in the Introduction) is simple; communication is not easy. The chance of misunderstanding is ever present between two people with different backgrounds, experience, intentions, prejudices and points of view. This may involve the different interpretation of one word – for example, just how fast is *immediately*? In terms of providing information, this may mean that someone will see to something when they are at their desk tomorrow morning and get the details in the post that day. But someone else might reasonably assume they will have the details by e-mail within the hour; more precision is needed to avoid this sort of clash. And that example relates to just one word: alternatively, it may be that a long, disjointed explanation of something that needs explaining ends up confusing rather than informing.

So the first rule is probably to be careful, not falling into the trap of thinking that communication is entirely straightforward, but making sure that you choose words carefully and make sure that you work at being clearly understood. Similarly, avoid repeating slavishly something to a list of people, all of whom may differ in their thinking sufficiently to need a different approach, one that reflects them and their situation. For example, if you are trying to recruit people to a committee the case you make to an older retired person may not convince someone younger and busier. Remember too that people are really impressed by good explanation: something that they expect to be complicated but which turns out to be straightforward. This is a good basis for giving a good impression, and for positioning yourself as knowledgeable and authoritative. What else helps guarantee that you achieve real understanding? I would mention four factors:

Structure

The logic of any message is crucial. This means taking things one at a time, in bite-sized pieces that you can deal with manageably and that the other person can comprehend, and flagging or 'signposting' what is being done. Thus something that begins, *You will want to know something about what we are trying to achieve, how you can help and what sort of time commitment is involved. Let's take your time commitment first, then* ... is likely to be followed more easily than something that just jumps in and deals with points at random. If someone knows what is coming and already sees it as being a sensible approach and likely to be what they want to hear, they will be more receptive. It also stops them taking mental digressions as they say, *Where's all this going?* Indeed knowing your initial thinking is clear and appropriate impresses and gives some advance credence to what is to come. The antithesis, what I call the 'and another thing' approach, where what is said is apparently at random and unprepared, and much less designed to be appropriate to the individual, is much less powerful and may fail to make a case at all.

Sequence

This goes logically with structure. There needs to be a clear and relevant sequence to the way that you go through something, and again you should make this clear to people in advance (as was done, for instance, early on in this book). For instance, if you are selling your house your estate agent (or you) needs to decide a logical route to show people around during a viewing, one that highlights key aspects of the property and links things together along the way. Every meeting, every conversation, needs thinking about, and organising, in this sort of way to make sure that one, two, three does not become two, three, one.

Visual (or sales) aids

Something visual always makes things easier to understand. An estate agent has the whole property to act as a visual aid, but very much simpler things can have the same effect. A picture is worth a thousand words the old saying has it, and there is a great deal of truth in it. A graph may make a point about cost-effectiveness in a moment, when it might otherwise take many minutes to explain; photographs, charts, brochures, all these will help you get your message over. Even showing a potential committee member a copy of the minutes of the last meeting may help: not because they read them, but because they can see that they are only a couple of neatly laid out pages and that says something about the meetings. See what items are available to hand. Create more if necessary; and use them. Again, more of this anon.

Description

Do not just tell people something; paint them a picture. Some people rarely use an adjective in describing a case, yet it is essential that people see what you mean. You must stir their imagination; perhaps saying, *This could just change your life*, rather than, *I think you will find this interesting.*

Using bland language dilutes persuasion, and dilutes the impression you want to give by default. Using it is not a very good approach – let me rephrase that: it is a disastrous approach that can kill the prospects of gaining agreement stone dead.

Any loose and inappropriate phraseology can dilute your message. A good example here links to figures: *nothing is about 10.7%*; it is either *about 10%* or you need to quote the exact figure. A phrase like *about 10.7%* will cast doubt on your numeracy and on every other figure you may use in your argument to bolster your case.

In presenting your case, this aspect rightly comes first; understanding is the foundation upon which the rest of the persuasion process rests.

Beware of jargon

Nothing dilutes understanding more easily than inappropriate use of jargon. Jargon has been called 'professional slang' and is particularly used in the context of technical matters. Between people of like understanding it can act as useful shorthand. Within my own firm no one has time to say *'all-comers' seminar'* (meaning a training event promoted by, say, a management institute and attended by people from several different organisations) so we say *'GT course'*. It stands for general training course – and no, I have no recollection of how or why its use started – but we all know what it means and using it saves a second or two. It is meaningless, however, to clients and such a phrase must not be used externally or it will cause confusion. What is worse, when this sort of thing does occur, you may not detect such confusion. People do not always react at once to such a phrase. They do not interrupt and ask what it means (not least because they may fear they should know and do not wish to appear stupid). They let it go by and hope the overall sense of what is being said will remain clear as the conversation progresses. But if this sort of thing happens very often, they do notice; and quite possibly their understanding is reduced, or they do get lost, have to ask and then resent the need to do so. Either way your credibility suffers.

So watch out for jargon, especially as for most people its use is a habit (if so, become a recovering jargonaholic as soon as possible). It comes in two varieties:

- •)) Corporate jargon.

- •)) Technical jargon.

Corporate jargon is that used within any organisation – formal or informal. It is such that I quoted above, and it often reduces things to sets of initials – these describe the products, systems, processes, people, departments, all the things to which reference is made often and where a shorthand description is therefore useful – *provided everyone understands it*. It does not need to be a large corporation. Small entities are just as liable to use jargon. For instance, my wife is involved in a hospital charity and if I see minutes of their meetings some of their content seems like a foreign language to me.

The technicalities of an industry or specialist area can also give rise to jargon; some more so than others. Computers and everything associated with them are a case in point, one with which we are probably all too familiar. The machine on which I prepared this book is a marvel of modern technology. But its manual has a nightmare lack of clarity. The language in it seems to be 90% jargon and assumes that the user has a particular level of understanding that makes this appropriate, despite it being perfectly possible to write most of it in plain English. This makes a good final point: the important thing with jargon is not so much to avoid all the technicalities, but to make sure – absolutely sure – that they are pitched at an appropriate level for those to whom you speak; each of them individually. In addition, some technical or quasi-technical phrases become so hackneyed that they lose all meaning. I once asked a friend in the computer world what exactly the phrase '*user friendly*' meant. He thought for a moment, then said: *I suppose it means it is very, very complicated, but not as complicated as next year's model!* Some descriptions just get past their sell-by date. Once upon a time, 'user friendly' might have been a neat description, but these days, when it has been repeatedly applied to every gadget in the whole universe, it fails to add any real power.

Every specialist area, however simple it seems to those in it, has its own jargon and a range of people to be dealt with at differing levels of technical competence; so an important thing here is to be on 'jargon-alert' as you speak and watch out that you do not inadvertently dilute the understanding you promote by letting inappropriate jargon slip in.

To use (but also explain!) some jargon of jargon: adopt a NUJA approach (that is: Never Use Jargon Automatically). Of course, it can be useful, but it may also dilute understanding and its use always needs some conscious thought.

Make what you say attractive

It is one thing to be understood; it is another to make your descriptions truly attractive so that people want to listen and are keen to let you complete the case you want to make. So, how do you do this?

You must talk *benefits* (okay, another jargon word, but I *will* explain).

Consider products and services: the base principle here is that customers do not buy products and services for what they *are*, they buy them for what the products or services *do for them or mean to them* – for their *benefits*. Many people know the phrase about *selling the sizzle and not the sausages,* and the head of a cosmetics company, Elizabeth Arden, is reputed to have said, rather less kindly, *I don't sell cosmetics. I sell hope.* Both statements link to this principle. To take a general example, people do not buy precision drills (what they are), but the ability to make precision holes (what drills will do); and they will only want that because of some deeper need, to repair the car or put up shelves. The benefits can range wide too. Different people may go on holiday, even to the same place, for very different reasons: for rest and relaxation, for adventure or activities, to explore new cultures and so on; and may do so for different background reasons too – to reward their hard work or impress the neighbours, perhaps. The principle is the same for anything: your boss will not give you that salary increase because of the amount of money it represents for you; they will do it because of what it does for them – perhaps believing it will retain you in the organisation longer (assuming they want that!) or increase your productivity.

This is probably the single most important tenet of successful persuasion; yet, the world over, there are many people talking predominantly about *features*, factual things about the item or issue, when they should be talking benefits. And, as a result, there are too many cases failing to be made as people with their eyes glazing over say to themselves *So what?* in response.

Talking benefits, and indeed leading your argument with benefits, is a key element in making what you say attractive. Doing so is not so very complicated; yet perhaps because it is counter-intuitive – we want to tell people *about* something; it is somehow most natural to talk about features – it can take conscious effort to state things the other way round.

So, the first task is to recognise which is which, feature or benefit, and it is useful to think through what you are discussing, listing benefits first and seeing how they link with features. Consider a simple product example: a particular car may have a five-speed gearbox (a feature); telling someone this may seem just like another piece of technical information prompting the response, mentally or verbally, *So what?* Worse, an inexperienced driver may worry that it is more complicated than they can manage. But, let us say that the sales person has identified a need for economy, then he or she can talk first about low fuel usage and money saved (both benefits), quoting the feature of the five-speed gearbox as a reason that makes that possible. Often one feature may, of course, link to more than one benefit. In the case of the car, reduced engine wear and smoother, quieter high-speed cruising may also result from there being a five-forward-speed gearbox rather than four. Try thinking this through with something a little more technical in mind (anti-lock braking system (ABS) brakes or torque, perhaps, in the case of the car) or applying it to your own situation.

All the descriptions you use can be handled in this way. And, as a result you should avoid the use of phrases that mean a lot to you, but which fail to explain the full meaning to someone else. For instance: imagine you want to move house. You must sell your own property and are trying to choose which estate agent to appoint. One estate agent may claim to have *wide coverage of the area*. Meaning what exactly – a very large flat office spread over an acre? No: what they would probably say, if made to extend the point, is that they have: *an extensive chain of offices, use all suitable newspapers to advertise locally (and maybe nationally as well), so that more people see the details, are prompted to make contact to obtain more information and arrange a viewing and that the chances of a sale, breaking the purchase chain and of your being able to move before the start of the next school term are high.* This is not suggested as the exact way they will say it, rather to make the point that the first short statement about wide coverage is actually only describing features. Only as it is explained – continuing the thought that begins with *which means that* – does the description turn to focus on benefits and become both inherently more interesting and more closely linked to the actual need of someone with a house to sell. The tendency to allow short statements to do the job of a better explanation is a very common fault, one that can ensure that the power to persuade is short-changed; beware when you have something to describe. Do not assume everyone else will interpret every word or phrase exactly as you do. Dwelling on the example a moment longer, the best sequence for the estate agent to use will put the benefit first, maybe: *We will maximise the likelihood of a quick sale, and maximise the number of people who see details by ...* then, as they describe how they will do that, they list the features.

Talking benefits in this way as you describe something is a vital part of the task of being persuasive. It is important to get it right; a

Chairperson should not say *being on the committee is 'worthwhile'*. No doubt it is, but the benefits to an individual who agrees to serve are more personal: it may give them a specific profile in the local community, allow them to meet certain (useful) people, or add meaning to a life in danger of becoming boring. The detail and amount to be said depends on the individual, of course, but essentially what being worthwhile means must be spelt out in terms of benefits.

Let us define another factor in play here: if you lead what you say with benefits, then features fall naturally into place as *what makes benefits possible*. The car offers good fuel economy, *because it has a five-speed gearbox*. Remember also that everyone is different, and in some cases you may need to be persuasive to a group of people who *all* have influence on a decision, as with a family group, a committee or a board of directors. In either case, people will have their own needs and agenda and benefits must be presented so that they relate to all the individual situations and points of view involved.

Relating benefits to individuals

The tailored nature of the approach that is often necessary has been mentioned before. Linked to talking benefits, it is a vital part of what can make you persuasive. It is one thing to define what the various benefits and features are, but that does not mean you have to throw every conceivable benefit about indiscriminately at everyone in the same way. Two things are important here: suitability and comprehensiveness.

- •)) **Suitability:** In the example of a car, fuel economy was shown as a benefit provided by the feature of a five-speed gearbox (though, for the record, this is not the only contributor to the level of fuel use, of course). However, the usefulness of this benefit depends on the individual customer actually being interested in economy. Someone buying a high-performance, prestige car such as a Ferrari might well not care how far it goes on a litre of fuel, though they could be interested in other benefits produced by the same feature – high-speed cruising being quieter and more comfortable in a fifth gear. So benefits must always be selected intelligently to match people's needs and priorities.

•)) **Comprehensiveness:** Overheard: Early on in a sales meeting the potential customer asked: *Perhaps you could give me some background about your company?* Certainly, came the reply, following which they did not appear to draw breath for 25 minutes. The sales person described chronologically the company history, its start, development, ups and downs, the people, customers, services – ad nauseam. Each piece of information was well described, everything that was said was true, but most of it was simply not relevant to the customer, who had probably expected 25 sentences, or even words, rather than 25 minutes. Comprehensiveness is never, or very rarely, an objective; whatever it is you are trying to be persuasive about, achieving comprehensiveness just takes far too long. Most people are busy and they expect you to concentrate on what is most important – to them. You must often have all sorts of information at your fingertips in terms of benefit, but you must then select from it, picking those benefits which you judge are most likely to make the case you want, and using those, in the right order and the right way, to achieve what you want and do so succinctly. Do this and your proposition will seem more attractive to more people.

•)) **Note:** At the same time any case must have sufficient weight in order to persuade. Just one reason, however beguiling, may fail to do the trick. Some interesting research seems to confirm this. It has been shown that five is the optimum number of benefits and makes success most likely. That does not mean that four or six are wholly inappropriate, taken as a guide to what gives a case significant weight; four to six main points seems about right. To be fair, the research applies in the commercial world and relates to businesses making formal presentations as part of what they do to produce business, but the point makes sense and has, I am sure, general application. (For the record, see: *Killer Presentations*, Nick Oulten, How to Books.)

Deploying different types of benefits

Another factor allows benefits to be deployed more precisely. There are three different types of benefit and each presents different opportunities to make your case appear truly attractive. Return to the thought of seeking a pay rise as an example.

- •)) **Benefits to the person (your boss) in their job:** They may want to know you will stay longer or be more productive and that this will help them achieve the objectives for their team and thus be able to meet their job objectives better.

- •)) **Benefits to the person as an individual:** They may feel that their personal relationship with you will be better, and so as a result will be your work (and that you will stop wasting time dropping hints).

- •)) **Benefits to others who are important to your boss:** If you work more effectively and performance increases, their boss will think well of them.

Using the full range of benefits available and relating them to all possible situations can increase the power of what you say. So too can combining this sort of statement into a logical sequence so that all the listener's needs are met.

For example, someone (that estate agent) might say: *The advertisement we recommend is 10 × 6 and includes a photograph (features). This means it is most likely to be seen and will give sufficient information to prompt enquiries (benefit). Thus you get viewers with a real interest coming along promptly and you increase your chances of a quick sale (benefit and need satisfaction).* Again there are various ways to phrase this; indeed, it might be more powerful still with the benefit leading: *To get viewers with a real interest coming along promptly and to increase your chances of a quick sale...*

The more you work with the concept of benefits, the more adept you will become at putting things in terms with which others will most readily identify. You can turn your thinking about anything into a form that reflects this concept. As a further example consider a wedding. The bride wants it to be memorable. This sounds easy to agree with, but saying that the gardens of a particular potential venue will allow wonderful photographs to be taken is more likely to persuade a proud father that it is worth paying more to gain this advantage.

Time and care spent on getting the core description of something right – focused on what it will *do for* the individual – is vital. Without this, any description will be pedestrian and unlikely to top any alternative offerings being considered; with it, you differentiate and create an immediate edge.

Throughout the conversation to date, your language must always match your intention. The boxed paragraph on pages 77–78 adds some further thoughts about this.

Language appropriate to persuasion

The overall tone of what you say, and the ways you use language as you try to persuade, are all important. So, to help prompt some thought about this and show how a benefit-led conversation should sound, here are some do's and don'ts.

- •)) **Avoid an introspective tone:** If every sentence, paragraph or thought begins with the word 'I' – *I will ... I can ...* and worst of all *I want*, it creates a 'catalogue' approach, a list of things from your own point of view, which becomes tedious and is not likely to prompt interest in whoever it is you are talking to. Try rephrasing any such sentiment, starting it with the word 'You'. It will sound very different. Thus: *I would like to point out ...* becomes something that begins *You will find* .... If the latter continues by explaining *why* people will find something interesting, better still.

- •)) **Avoid circumspection:** A persuasive message is no place for *I think – I hope – probably – maybe* or *perhaps*. You need to be positive and have the courage of your convictions. Ideas and suggestions, or anything for which you seek agreement, must reflect your confidence in it. So phrases like *This will give you ...* are better. Similarly avoid bland description. Your idea is never just *very good*. A suggested feature should never be stated as being quite interesting. Use words that add drama and certitude.

- •)) **Stress the benefits:** As has been said, this reflects some of the jargon of the sales world. Features are factual things – tangible or intangible – about something. If I say that this whole book is about 45,000 words long, occupies about 170 pages and deals with the techniques of persuasion: all these descriptions are features. Whereas benefits are things that something does for or means to people. So the benefits of reading this are things like: giving you an introduction to the principles of making messages persuasive, helping you avoid key mistakes that will dilute the persuasive effectiveness of your approach or increasing the chances of your next proposition being accepted. Benefits should predominate. They should be sufficient to persuade, they should be well expressed and, if necessary, backed up by proof or evidence (that is something other than you saying so).

•)) **Make what you say flow:** Like anything else, you will need a clear beginning, middle and end, no labrynthine explanations and a shining clarity throughout. In context here it is often important to allow how you put something over to project something of yourself. Make sure it is not formulaic as if you wrote out the best way of expressing it and are reading it out. If you want to sound friendly, efficient or professional, make sure such characteristics show in your voice and add to how persuasive you are.

Make what you say credible

In defining persuasion, the third element mentioned was the need to make what is said convincing – credible to the listener. It is a fact that often many people have some inherent scepticism towards anyone being persuasive; why else do we say, 'I wouldn't buy a second-hand car from them' and use it as an insult? People believe that the persuader is likely to have a vested interest; they believe that they need to be sceptical and, if a good point is made about something, their first reaction may be to think: *They would say that, wouldn't they?* (a reaction known to those who remember the Profumo affair as the 'Mandy Response'). So, understandably enough, they want proof.

The main form of evidence, certainly the one that builds in best to the benefit-orientated conversation you should be conducting, is the features. Benefits followed by features focuses on the other person and offers linked proof, so as touched on earlier, in a statement such as: *This model will give you the low fuel consumption you want and reduce your motoring costs, because it has a five-speed gearbox.* There is factual, physical proof here; someone can see and touch the gear lever, and is reassured that it really exists and it is not just a sales ploy. Such proof may be asked for and, even if it is not, it should be built into the argument you put across as it is an inherent requirement if you are to be persuasive. Never rely solely on your own argument; build some real proof into the case you present.

More proof may be needed than can be provided by features alone, and, in particular, people may demand, or appreciate, something from some outside sources, independent of whomever they are dealing with and, if there is one, their organisation. Here you may need to do some assembling of the kind of point that can be made to offer such *external* proof. There are different independent authorities to be quoted in different fields. For instance, all the following are sources of independent opinion and thus provide proof.

- •)) An award of some sort received by, say, a restaurant (though a CD that got to the top of the charts shows the range of things involved here).

- •)) A link with another respected entity: between a surveyor and an insurance company or an architect and a planning consultant.

- •)) Sales figures may have this impact: the estate agent with the greatest number of sales in the area (or the amount a charity lunch raised, quoted as you try to get a sponsor for the next event).

- •)) Experience: twenty years' involvement in something (and the time can be independently checked) may well mean something in terms of quality or reliability.

•))) Positive editorial comment in the press and other media.

Just to give one example, a good write-up in the local newspaper about a fundraising event might well influence someone to join a committee to help with the next one. You can probably think of more examples, and you need to think systematically about any case you plan to make so as to assemble all possible proof factors that can then be kept in mind to be selected and used when appropriate.

A further, and sometimes more powerful, form of proof is that of testimonials or references: in other words, evidence of past successful experience. A company making even general mention of the kinds of people they already deal with to a potential new buyer can add reassurance. Specific past names quoted may be more useful than just a hint of 'someone'. For this they may need to get permission so that they can say, *Patrick Forsyth is a regular user of our services*. And such people or organisations need to be selected carefully. Quoting to a small company that you do business with several large multinationals may put them off, and vice versa. Similarly if you quote a company, which is competitive with another, this may just annoy them; and, if they are so dissimilar that they feel they do not compare, this may add nothing to the argument. So, for the committee, different existing members might be quoted to several potential new recruits. Whatever reference of this sort is used must be quoted in the belief that it will impress – *if that is the case, this must be good*.

Look at this with the example of the presentation in mind again. Credibility might be added in various ways.

•))) Quoting past experience: *the project approach is very like … and that worked well.*

•))) Involving the support of others (a person or organisation): *the Training Manager says a rehearsal would be useful* (when the other party respects the person referred to).

•)) Quoting measurement of results: *50% of this kind of presentation end without securing agreement; let's make this one of the successful ones.*

•)) Mentioning any guarantees, tests or standards that are met: *we must not overrun and this will help ensure we keep to time.*

•)) Invoking quantity that reinforces the case: *several of our colleagues work this way* (then maybe focusing on one example).

The right supporting evidence of all sorts, fielded in the right way, is powerful in adding credibility to a case and to strengthening differentiation. Have the right evidence ready and use it wisely, and if circumstances permit make sure it is something external and tangible. If the salesman says the car will do 50 mpg, do you believe him? Or would it carry more weight if he said that independent tests (which he quotes) say that it does so? I suspect there is no contest for most of us and, if such works for us, similar things will work for those we aim to persuade. Thus perhaps the Chairperson should not say that being a serving member takes about four hours a month; he might better say, *John's been a member for a year or so now, and he tells me he finds it takes up about four hours a month.*

Beyond these three key elements, which together can contribute so much to persuasion, there are various further techniques that are useful to ensure that putting over your case during a meeting goes well.

Checking progress

The stage of any dialogue when you are describing your case is one when, perhaps necessarily, you will be doing most of the talking; but you should not be doing it all. You need to have some feedback as matters progress to check that you are on target. It is easy to let your enthusiasm for getting across your message make you talk uninterrupted, yet people do not value a monologue so much as a conversation in which they are involved. Indeed, anything else breeds suspicion. They appreciate your checking periodically to see whether you still have their interest, whether they understand and whether what you are saying continues to be relevant to them.

This is something easily done, in part, by observation. Some obvious signs of acceptance or rejection you will see at once, provided you look for them. Nods, expressions and a person's manner will all provide clues as to what reaction you are getting. But you need more than this; your conversation has to include checks such as: *Does that make sense?* or *Should I give you more details of that?* Such questions need not be complicated, and if some of them are *open questions* – that is they cannot be answered with a simple yes or no – then you will obtain actual comment as to how they are feeling. Asking, for example, *How well does what I am saying tie in with the kind of approach you have in mind?* Not only is the feedback valuable, the information provided is like having a hand on the tiller in a boat, enabling gentle changes of course as the voyage progresses and as wind and tide change along the way. The whole process improves the accuracy of what you do and the likelihood of agreement resulting from it.

Summarise progress

Perhaps an extension of checking progress is provided by the technique of summarising. This is always useful, but the longer a meeting is, and the more complicated it may be, the greater the need is to keep it well organised. If you are directing the meeting and proceeding in a clear, structured manner, then people should keep up with the argument; however, summarising briefly as you go along will help make sure everything remains clear throughout. You do not want to give the impression of extending the meeting unnecessarily, but you do need to recap occasionally, especially on topics that are important. This can be done as a help to both parties and signposted as exactly what it is: *Let me just summarise at this point. It seems there are three main criteria that have to be met: first, ...* Or you can just make it a part of the conversation. In either case it will help you keep the meeting on track and it also acts usefully to help you keep things straight in your own mind. Keep people with you in this way; it can help keep them with you right up to the moment they say, yes.

Adding something visual

In the world of selling, a 'sales aid' is any physical element used to enhance what is said and make an explanation clearer or a point more powerful. Here we consider the use of this sort of thing in a wider context and, if 'sales aid' is an inappropriate description let's call them 'case enhancers', because that is what they are intended to do. But first, consider – how do you store them? In a word: carefully. So many times I have seen people who have either not been able to find something they have said they will show and which they intend to use to add weight to an argument, or who have pulled an item from a briefcase that looks as if it contains the aftermath of a small explosion – hardly the way to appear professional. Such inefficiency will be noticed and all such aids are important. They deserve to be looked after properly.

Any case enhancer deserves to be used correctly and the golden rule is simple: you must let them speak for themselves. If there are two things many people find difficult in meetings, they are being patient and keeping silent. And the good use of aids demands both. For example, imagine you are trying to persuade a friend to help you with some DIY task: to assemble something perhaps where an extra pair of hands would help. You have what you believe to be clear instructions, and feel the existence of these will make agreement to help more likely, but their use still demands a systematic approach:

•)) The instructions must first be *introduced*. This introduction should explain why it is being shown, in other words what it will help explain to the person – and why *they* will find it helpful.

•)) Then you *show* the instructions. And you wait while they look at them. You wait until your friend's attention comes back to you from the picture, plans or whatever, because, if the thing is of any interest at all, then when it is put in front of them they will want to look at it, will do just that and doing so will take their attention. No one can look at something, concentrate on it, and listen to you at the same time. So you wait. And the more complex or the more interesting it is, the longer you must remain waiting silently. This may seem a simple point, but because it can seem awkward to keep silent there is a great temptation to chip in and continue the conversation. But if you do, and if what you say makes an important point, you may succeed only in distracting from the visual image and yet not do so sufficiently for someone to take in the point you have just made. After a moment's hiatus the conversation resumes and not as good a total point has been made as you would have wished. This scenario is made more complicated if you have, say, complicated plans to go through: every time you turn over a page then you must wait for them to take in what they see and for their attention to return to you.

•)) Then you *remove* them, so that they do not distract as you continue speaking (promising to leave a copy, come back to them or whatever is appropriate) and continue the conversation.

The effect of seeing something during a conversation is powerful. It makes things easier to understand. And when it does, this, of course, is likely to be noticed and valued. It helps paint a picture, and it can save time – again a commodity that many people will doubtless value. It also adds variety to the meeting and this too helps maintain concentration.

Furthermore, such items can appear very personalised. Something may be shown as what is clearly part of standard material. Nothing wrong with that; it will be expected if such a thing is logical and someone may well like what they see and find it useful. But there is sometimes an opportunity for material to create a different impression by being (or sometimes seeming to be) tailored just for this one occasion. Back to your friendly potential DIY helper: maybe there are no instructions, but you have written something out or drawn a diagram. Its personalised nature may then be apparent from the description you use: *Knowing we would need to talk through how to go about it, I prepared a diagram that will* …. In many contexts if someone sees that something has been provided specially for them, they appreciate it more. It does not simply help to explain; it can develop and build the relationship between the two parties.

Good items like this can make people find a meeting or conversation memorable. It pays dividends to make sure that you have an adequate number of them, that they are good quality and appropriate – that they are genuinely helpful to people – and to use them carefully and effectively.

Note: So important is it to get things right in this area – the right aids, appropriately organised – that in any repetitive situation you may find it useful to list what you plan to use on a checklist. List the items you have to deploy, and link them to such factors as:

- •)) The situation they best relate to.

- •)) What aspect of what you will say they illustrate.

- •)) Proof that what you say is true.

Remember that anything can be used. I once met a sales engineer who sold mining equipment (drills the size of a small car). In meetings he produced from a large pilot case a large, extremely heavy chunk of rock. One side of it was cut as when a knife goes through butter into a shiny flat surface, and he had a wonderful tale about the rock being the hardest granite in the world. It certainly made a point to anyone not able to descend a mine shaft and inspect his equipment in situ. When you think what you might use in this kind of way, cast your net wide, think creatively and exclude nothing that might help.

Do not exaggerate

This is a most important maxim. Never, ever exaggerate. Nothing switches people off more quickly than obvious over-exaggeration; do not be tempted to do it. One phrase too many and your credibility collapses around you; in fact, of all the mistakes you can make in persuasion, this is certainly... but, you are right, I am exaggerating. Though I hope to make a point ... and it is important.

Seriously, credibility is a fragile flower and a good case can very easily be diluted by something that positions you as going 'over the top'. If you have a good case, by all means say so, but give reasons for excellence and spend more time talking more about what something does for or means to someone than about simply the fact that it is good. Beware particularly of superlatives. If you say something is '*the best*', then you must be able to back it up. Too strident a description from which you have to climb down: *Well, when I say best, I mean undoubtedly one of the best* ... will dilute any good impression you may initially have achieved. Remember the scepticism with which much of what anyone with 'something to sell' is received, and that people may well question each statement, asking themselves whether it should be taken at face value, whether it is to be believed and deciding whether the overall case being presented is becoming stronger or weaker. Finally, remember also – a common mistake – that few things are 'unique' (a much overused word meaning literally like nothing else). This means that saying something is quite, very or entirely 'unique' is simply grammatically incorrect and a misuse of a useful word, one which can be powerful when correctly used. There is a chance here too that some people will notice such mistakes, but not take on board the points that are being made; again the results dilute effectiveness.

Do not pressurise

People like to make considered judgements. Pressure to make a decision before they have completed what they regard as the necessary thinking process, weighing up the pros and cons of a potential decision, will often have the reverse effect of that desired. It will increase their resolve to think it through and not to be rushed. People usually read undue pressure in three ways.

- •)) Insensitivity to their point of view (this is particularly bad because one of the things they often positively seek as a characteristic of someone they respect is an understanding of them and their point of view).

- •)) A smoke screen, at worst one specifically designed to disguise some weakness in your case, which you apparently feel will show itself in time, hence the inappropriate rush to close the deal.

- •)) As desperation, which might have all sorts of causes – none of which inspires confidence, or makes you appear anything but unprofessional.

So go for a successful outcome by all means, push hard, be persistent and have and display the courage of your convictions, but do not put undue pressure on people in a way that will be obvious and which will be read as unprofessional, especially if doing so is an alternative to using the more positive techniques reviewed here. Be particularly careful of this when there is a genuine need to hurry.

Demonstrating effectively

Not everything lends itself to demonstration, but some things do (if nothing you want to be persuasive about has this aspect to it, by all means skip on, though all sorts of things have this connotation: I watched, fascinated by how closely it paralleled persuasive communication, at my sailing club recently as someone demonstrated how to raise and lower the sails as part of the overall task of persuading a youngster that they could manage to take a boat out single handed).

Where called for, an effective demonstration can strengthen what is said considerably, and is another area to potentially heighten differentiation. Seeing is believing. There is no substitute for someone actually having the evidence of their own eyes to back up what is said to them. But demonstrations must be approached in the right way; they must be effective and that means 100 per cent effective. Anything less simply does not meet the need.

An effective demonstration starts with prior consideration about the demonstration's audience. It may be to one person; it may be to several. A group situation illustrates some of the problems of a formal presentation. You may feel exposed standing in front of an expectant group, and thinking beforehand about what you will say and how you will make it go smoothly and in a way that will boost your self-confidence. Each person in this sort of situation may have a different agenda and be looking for, and potentially swayed by, different points. So depending on who is involved and what their situation, current experience and knowledge of something is, you need to proceed accordingly.

Let us take selling a house again as an example (it could be a house that is for sale or rent). To do it successfully needs preparation. Whatever you are showing needs to be well presented. You need all the facts at your fingertips: for instance if asked how many power points there are in the sitting room, do you know? You need to say, *Six: two doubles and two singles* or whatever; anything that starts, *I'm not sure* or *I think* dilutes the air of confidence that you display.

What are the key factors? Well, many of the basic rules of persuasion apply: you must focus on the other person, maintain interest (not everything may be of the same level of interest and a tour should dwell on those things that will be appreciated most. For example, a couple expecting a baby might give special attention to a likely nursery), go through matters to a pre-explained structure and sequence and, above all, talk benefits. The job is to get people to imagine the place in use (the classic general example here is a car – and a test drive which allows someone to imagine owning and driving it; viewing a house has a similar connotation). With that in mind, remember the following points.

- •))) **Set up fast:** Make sure you get everything ready in time: is the house tidy or are things you want to demonstrate accessible?

- •))) **Make it understandable:** This is vital. Tours can be spoilt by jargon, gobbledegook and confusion; a lengthy discussion about details of construction or decoration that have little interest, perhaps. Everything must be spelt out so that it is crystal clear. Finding it easy to understand will be read as a good sign, and prompts to imagination can quickly build up a powerful picture – *which of the children would you see having this room?*

- •))) **It must work!** If there is nowhere to park, the key does not fit a lock or you get an electric shock when you turn on a light, then from the point of view of the person viewing you have a problem, and quite right too. The overall experience must be smooth as silk.

- •))) **Make them feel how it could be:** Everything must be done not just so that they 'get a feeling for the place' in a general sense, but also so that they can truly imagine how it could be to live or work in it. The detail is important here – you do not want people, on their own later, not appreciating that there was space for the washing machine or something else crucial. This applies even if 'could be' needs taking literally, with a viewing of one room accompanied by the comment, *Imagine the size this would be with that wall removed.*

•))) **Project what you want:** And what they want. If the tour must demonstrate comfort or quirkiness or ease of maintenance and potential for expansion, then make sure such prime messages come over.

Throughout the process the emphasis is perhaps on proof. You are not just talking about it: you can show it, they can try or experience it – and always seeing is believing.

You must work to ensure everything is exactly as you want. There are very few second chances in persuasion and in few parts of the overall process is this truer than when showing something in this way. Time spent beforehand to make sure that you get it right is always time very well spent.

Making terms and conditions clear

Some agreements have contractual terms of varying degrees of complexity attached to them. These can be complicated or simply something like the election processes that may go with serving on a committee. Sometimes there are factors involved here, which people do not like, however much they understand the necessity for them; perhaps the formality puts them off. Because there can be a perceived difficulty in introducing such topics, it is easy when persuasion is the order of the day to avoid facing such issues: the thinking tends to be that it is better first to concentrate on obtaining agreement and then worry about any terms of agreement that may be involved. But this can cause problems. People can then feel that issues have been disguised or avoided rather than delayed; so certainly in a business context you may need a clear policy as to how you deal with such issues. This very much needs to be tailored, every organisation is different in the way terms operate, but some general pointers may still be useful.

The existence and use of any terms and conditions must protect and regulate the transaction and remove the possibility of problems in the longer term. Thus if we persuade someone to give us a complimentary loan of a hall for a charity event, they may still want us to sign a cancellation arrangement so that they are not left unable to fill it if we cancelled at the last minute. Fair enough. At the same time it is important that any terms:

- •)) Are communicated clearly and prevent misunderstandings.

- •)) Project efficiency.

- •)) Enhance the relationship between people (and thus be seen as acceptable and necessary).

- •)) Encourage agreement effectively and promptly.

- •)) Link to any other necessary arrangements and documentation.

In discussing terms and conditions, never apologise for their necessity. Stress the *mutual* advantages, talk about working together and, if complexity makes it necessary, use a checklist to ensure you deal with everything systematically. Specifically you may want to evolve a step-by-step way of introducing, describing and making terms and conditions stick. The following sequence illustrates the kind of progression involved.

- •)) **Introduce the concept of contractual agreement:** You need to consider the timing of this in particular circumstances, but it is usually best early on rather than later; and though details may be left over, it is important to make it clear that 'contract' means something confirmed in writing. Remember the moment passes; it may get progressively more difficult to introduce contractual matters later once it has been left too long. Do not wait for the other person to raise the issue. They are unlikely to do so.

•))) **Make clear the detail:** You must be careful to spell out accurately the detail and should not assume that anyone is familiar with everything – even if they have dealt with you previously. For example, expenses for a committee member: such things as travel costs must be clearly stated (first class or second on the train, for instance).

•))) **Stress particularly figures and timing:** There must be no misunderstanding about the details which, in the worst scenario, can cause the greatest problem. For example, are costs inclusive of tax? When is, 'in a month's time' exactly? (four weeks or …?). Deal with all the details thoroughly and carefully.

•))) **Check understanding:** This may be as simple as an occasional, *Is that clear?* but is very important. It is no good, at a later stage, believing everything was straight between you – you need to know.

•))) **Document your side of arrangements:** Tell people what you will do, and follow it up efficiently and promptly in a way that sets the pattern for clarity with written confirmation. And make it easy for people. Administrative chores breed delay, and people may prefer you to summarise details of a discussion so that they can write a couple of lines that say, *That's right, I agree.* The reverse will take longer. This may be checklist led; in other words, the details that need to be documented come off an agreed checklist document which acts as a prompt and reminder; it can be all too easy to overlook apparently small details.

•))) **Ask for confirmation:** Whatever it is you want, written confirmation, a signed contract, (as circumstances dictate) – you need to ask, specifically ask, for it. It is not necessary to go 'round the houses'; you do not need to make an issue of it (given your explanations, the person will, after all, see what is happening as an arrangement that needs documenting and will not be surprised). But you do need to make the process, and implications, clear and get it under way.

•)) **Record the action:** Keep a clear note of what you have done, how someone has responded and – most important – when it needs checking and when further action is needed. This should clearly link to follow-up diary systems or a note of some sort.

•)) **Chase for action:** This is crucial. If someone ignores key stages, and some will, you must actively remind them of their commitment. Do not feel awkward about doing this; after all you should be following up agreed commitments: *when will you let me have the contract back?* 'By the end of the week.' So people will expect it, and besides the penalty for delay can be very damaging. Such chasing must therefore always be systematic, courteous, but insistent.

•)) **Adopt the appropriate manner:** Throughout the process make it clear that this is not a negative procedure; indeed, ultimately it can be presented as a protection for both parties. So it is best to deal with it in a way that is efficient, that is professional and, if necessary, positions you as an appropriate point of contact from the other person's viewpoint.

•)) **Link to follow-up:** The contractual arrangement may link to all stages of the conversation and those beyond.

There are two further matters to consider here. The first is when payments are involved and we must ensure payment is made.

•)) **Invoicing:** Here it is most important that the invoice reflects – accurately – the agreed detail (finding that this is not the case is certain to cause friction), and is straightforward and clear. This may best be submitted with a personalised covering note. Sending the invoice, of course, implies chasing to get it paid. Again not an easy – or palpable – task, but it must be done and it is frankly easier to follow up in a way that gets it seen as a routine, rather than only when so much time has gone by that the approach must be heavy. This is vital (one of my first experiences of sales work was being told – *It's not a sale* *until the money is in the bank.* Wise advice, even if I digress somewhat).

•)) **Future contact:** If ongoing contact is involved, perhaps as a relationship is forged, we want the contractual side to become easier. Next time the procedure is 'as before', and if all went well this will be seen by the other person as reasonable, straightforward and hassle-free.

Anything contractual is an important area to deal with effectively. It is an integral part of some agreements. If delayed, skimped or ignored, it will certainly cause problems. Contracts and terms are, after all, primarily for when things go wrong; it is only then that many need to turn to the 'letter of the law'. Get this area right and it provides a firm basis for easy agreement.

Do not sound egocentric

To a degree, setting out to get agreement involves an egocentric approach. You have to think of it as *your* meeting. You want – indeed intend – it to be successful. You have to go for the objective, and that is always ultimately to obtain agreement so that you get your own way. All true and necessary, yet this approach should not show inappropriately and must not show overtly in your language.

So, do not prefix things you say by, for example: *If you want my opinion* ..., or *If I were you, I would* ... It too easily sounds patronising (and reminds me of an old boss of mine who used to say, *When I want your opinion, I'll give it to you.* Sorry, I digress). People may well be interested in your advice, but they expect it to be relevant to them, and based on some real consideration of their circumstances. Much better to lead into comments with something like: *For someone in your position the best approach is often* ..., or, *Given what you said about timing, we might best deal with it by* ....

People want to know, and to recognise clearly, that you are acting on their behalf and that what you say has their interests in mind; your opinion in isolation they can do without. You will find a conscious line of avoiding egocentric-sounding phraseology gives the best impression, and helps position you as someone of some weight.

Always be loyal to others

If you represent an entity of some sort – a company, association or committee – you will win acceptance more easily if people have not only a good relationship with you, but also a good image of whatever it is that you represent. In the world of business, many firms spend a great deal of money creating a good background image through public relations, design and other techniques. It is easy to undo this good work in a moment.

Imagine that in the course of discussion you are faced with a complaint because of a missed deadline. It is not your fault, the timing was clear, but someone else has made a mistake (the committee secretary or someone elsewhere in an organisation) and, for someone relying on the arrangement, this has understandably caused upset. We are all concerned to protect our personal image and reputation and it is easy to say something along the lines of: *You will appreciate it was out of my hands. I don't know how many times I have told those people how important it is to meet timing commitments, but they still seem to have got it wrong …* If you complete the sentence with the word 'again', the damage is made worse, and in either case the other person is left feeling that, however good their contact with you, the people or organisation behind you is less than efficient. What may have been intended to bolster your image ends up doing the reverse, when just saying, *I'm sorry* might have worked much better (saying so does not necessarily imply acceptance of personal blame if you simply speak on behalf of a body or organisation of some sort).

You may on occasion need to support policy set by others (even when you disapprove of it), defend colleagues who are less efficient than yourself and positively work at building the image of whoever you represent. People may well understand that no organisation is perfect, but one that seems to hold itself in low regard is seen as dubious – *If that is all they think of themselves,* they may think, *how can I have confidence in what they will do for me?* It is easy to let the wrong kind of description slip through, and, if it becomes a habit, then the damage may be considerable. Boost the image of others at every opportunity; even when you have to sort out difficulties, it can smooth the path for what follows and make what you do in persuasion just a little more certain. In this position you need to take it on the chin: *We do seem to have fallen down there, let's see ...,* commenting in a way that does not seem to be you avoiding blame and moving quickly on to what can be done to put things right.

Offer more

The advice in this book relates primarily to matters you will have the power to implement. Here, if you represent an organisation of some sort, then you may be dependent on company or central policy and have to take that into account in what you offer. Yet the principle here is an important and powerful aid to increasing the power of the case you make, so it deserves a mention.

You can increase the likelihood of success by offering more: more than usual, more than someone else, more than expected. Both in terms of tangible and intangible things. Many of the ways that spring to mind are temporary (they have less impact once they are permanent and taken for granted) and, with a business hat on, might be best described as promotional. We are all familiar with this sort of thing as we shop. For example, retailers may offer:

- •))) A free sample or trial of something.

- •))) A free element of product.

- •))) A limited or exclusive offer.

- •))) A saving, avoiding a coming price increase, an additional one-off discount, and more (one particular form of this has entered the language – the bogof: Buy One, Get One Free).

- •)) A higher specification for the cost of the basic offering.

- •)) An incentive (a gift, a trip, a competition).

- •)) Trade-in allowances for upgrading what is bought.

- •)) Better-than-usual credit terms.

- •)) Special guarantees.

- •)) Discounts or other rewards linked to future purchase.

Intangible factors may be involved here too. For instance, people: a professional firm might promise to, *put John in as project leader; he worked with you successfully previously.* A past customer might not doubt the competences of others but still prefer to work with someone they know and trust. I saw the same thing done at a gym to sign someone up on a new course, the other day. Although such things are by no means applicable or appropriate on every occasion, any of these and more can act to increase sales success. Generally such devices act in a number of different ways:

- •)) They help you get a hearing, perhaps for the first time.

- •)) They help improve the weight of the case you can present.

- •)) They can pull commitment forward, persuading people to agree now rather than later.

- •)) They can increase the size of a commitment.

- •)) They can affect the frequency of agreement.

They can also have negative effects, reducing the seeming importance of other benefits; or, in retailing, encouraging people to shop around, and only buy in turn from whoever is currently offering the best deal (and we know this occurs – we all do it to some extent). Any offer must form an organised, integrated part of your case. For a company such promotional offers must link to marketing strategy as they can affect image and profitability and cash flow. Some you may feel would work well in your situation, in which case you may want to incorporate them into what you do. Such ploys are undeniably useful, but you should never rely on them to the exclusion of making a sound case for agreement in other ways.

Now, can I persuade you to join a committee? If you do, then I will: guarantee not to get you involved taking minutes/let you attend a trial meeting before you make a final decision/accept that your involvement is just to get us over the next twelve months (I am sure we can find a permanent member by then)/arrange for you to get a lift to meetings so that you do not tie up the use of the family car. Even the simplest situations may be one where this device can be used in some form; it is worth a thought.

Putting it in writing

While being persuasive, in terms of its individual elements, is pretty much common sense, there is more than enough to it to create some real complexity. Something that certainly complicates matters is when a persuasive message must be put in writing: into a letter (or e-mail) or something longer. Too much detail, certainly about making the language persuasive, is beyond our brief here, though I have written at greater length about it in a business context in *How to Write Reports & Proposals* (Kogan Page). The most important thing is to keep it simple, by opting for short words, short sentences and short paragraphs. Do not let phrases become unnecessarily verbose, for instance writing *At this moment in time*, when you mean *Now*. Beyond that and using sufficient punctuation, the checklist of do's and don'ts that follow are adapted from the above book and, without digressing too much, provide some further useful thoughts about written communication.

The don'ts

You should **not**:

•)) **Be too clever:** It is the argument that should win the reader round, not your flowery phrases, elegant quotations or clever approach (though good description does help).

•)) **Be too complicated:** The point about simplicity has been made. It applies equally to the overall argument.

•)) **Be pompous:** This means saying too much about you, and (if it applies) about your organisation if there is one (instead of focusing on how what you are saying relates to the reader). It means writing in a way that is too far removed from the way you would speak. It means following too slavishly the exact grammar at the expense of an easy, flowing style.

•)) **Overclaim:** While you should certainly have the courage of your convictions, too many superlatives can become self-defeating. Make one claim that seems doubtful and the whole argument will suffer.

•)) **Offer opinions:** Or at least not too many compared with the statement of facts – ideally, substantiated facts.

•)) **Lead into points with negatives:** For example, do not say, *If this is not the case we will ...*, rather *You will find ... or ....*

•)) **Assume your reader lacks knowledge:** Rather than saying, for example, *You probably do not know that* .... You are better to say *Many people have not yet heard* .... Or: *Like others, you probably know ....*

•)) **Overdo humour:** Never use humour unless you are very sure of its success. An inward groan as they read does rather destroy the nodding agreement you are trying to build. A quotation or quip, particularly if it is relevant, is safer and even if the humour is not appreciated, the appropriateness may be noted.

•))) **Use up benefits early:** A persuasive document must not run out of steam: it must end on a high note and still be talking in terms of benefits even towards and at the end.

The do's

You should **do** the following:

•))) **Concentrate on facts:** The case you put over must be credible and factual. A clear-cut *these are all the facts you need to know* approach tends to pay particular dividends.

•))) **Use captions:** While pictures, illustrations, photographs and charts can often be regarded as speaking for themselves, they will have more impact if used with a caption. (This can be a good way of achieving acceptable repetition, with a mention in the text and in the caption.)

•))) **Use repetition:** Key points can appear more than once, for example in a letter and an accompanying report or attachment of some sort, even appearing more than once, with different phraseology, within the letter itself. This applies, of course, especially to benefits repeated for emphasis.

•))) **Keep changing the language:** You need to find numbers of ways of saying the same thing in any lengthy written message.

•))) **Say what is new:** Assuming you have something new, novel – even unique – to say, make sure the reader knows it. Real differentiation can often be lost, so in the quantity of words make sure that the key points still stand out.

•))) **Address the recipient(s):** You must do this accurately and precisely. You must know exactly to whom you are writing, something of their situation, likes and dislikes, and be ever conscious of making the message suitably individual. Going too far towards being all things to all people will dilute the effectiveness to any one recipient, even sometimes with something close-knit like a committee.

•)) **Keep them reading:** Consider breaking sentences at the end of a page so that readers have to turn over to complete the sentence. (Yes, it does not look quite so neat, but it works.) Always make it clear that other pages follow, putting 'continued ...' or something similar at the foot of the page.

•)) **Link paragraphs:** This is another way to keep them reading. Use 'horse and cart' points to carry the argument along. For example, one paragraph starts *One example of this is ...*; the next starts *Now let's look at how that works ....*

•)) **Be descriptive:** Really descriptive. Remember, you may know how good what you are describing is, but initially your readers do not. You need to tell them and you must not assume they will catch your enthusiasm from a brief phrase. In a written message, the words on the page are the only guide.

•)) **Involve people:** First your people. Do not say, *Another member of the committee* say, *John Smith, who joined a year or so ago.* And other people. Do not talk about *lots of sponsors* but say, *320 people sponsored our last fundraising event.*

•)) **Add credibility:** For example, if you quote people, quote names (with their permission). If you quote figures, quote them specifically. Being specific adds to credibility, so do not say, *Mary described this on page 3 of our newsletter ....*

•)) **Use repetition:** Key points can appear more than once, in a letter or an accompanying report or attachment of some sort, even appearing more than once, in different phraseology, within the letter itself. This applies, of course, especially to benefits repeated for emphasis. You will notice this paragraph is repeated (third bullet point on the previous page), either to show that the technique works or perhaps to demonstrate that some half-hearted attempts at humour are not altogether recommended!

Putting things in writing, and doing so poorly, will always dilute effectiveness and may make a message seem stilted. Always approach written things with care and aim for real precision. Remember that written messages last – and may come back to haunt you later, sometimes much later.

Enough, for the moment: there are still more things to consider, which influence success. But here in the core of the persuasive conversation there is clearly a good deal to think about (hence the long chapter). Furthermore, even if you get all this right, and things are going well, there can still be other problems. People may listen carefully, nod encouragingly, but still raise objections.

There is so often a but.

All the detail here is important and much of it stems from the premise that persuading must make your message: understandable, attractive and credible. While details in each of these areas can act to strengthen a case, it is when all three are incorporated and blended together that a case begins to have real power.

CHAPTER 5

Responding to People's Objections

Every setback is the starting point for a comeback.

Anon

All may be going well, you feel you are making an unarguable case and yet when you pause hoping for agreement the first thing you hear starts with the little word, 'But'. Let us be clear: objections are an inherent part of any kind of persuasive process. They spring directly from the human nature involved in what is being done and, whatever you are doing, you can be sure there will likely be some. When people raise them it is not necessarily a sign that there is any problem; indeed, it can be a positive sign of some interest on their part. By and large people do not bother taking time to query things when they have no interest in the overall case whatsoever. There is an old saying that *he who findeth fault meaneth to buy;* quite so. Handling objections is therefore an inherent part of the process. If this part is done well, it does not only redress the balance, or remove the objection entirely, its being well handled will itself be impressive – and that helps too. People like dealing with other people who, as they might put it, *'know their stuff'*. The smooth handling of objections is taken as a sign of confidence and competence. Not that you will always be able to remove them. There is no merit in trying to persuade people that black is white if it is, in fact, as black as pitch (or even if it is distinctly grey), and the last thing you want is to prompt an argument.

Rebalancing is what counts, as the points in this chapter describe.

Taking the positive view

Some people say objections are a sign of interest, and this is certainly a good way to regard them. Certainly you should expect to receive them. As we have seen, the way people go about making decisions is to weigh up the pros and cons. They expect to find some things on the downside (think of going to the shops: few things we buy are perfect; indeed, we may be suspicious if something is so described!). You should watch, however, for the quantity of objections you get. Too many can be a sign that it is your fault. By this I mean that with experience you will know roughly how much objection will be raised in a given situation, and to some extent what issues are likely to be involved. If you find that someone in a kind of persuasive encounter that you have regularly is raising more objections than you expect, then it may be that:

- •)) You have failed to identify sufficiently accurately what their situation and perception is and that what you are saying is therefore off target. More questions may correct this.

- •)) You are making suggestions too soon. People who feel their situation is unique or who expect a tailored recommendation may feel that what you are saying should follow more thought about them on your part.

- •)) You may (albeit inadvertently) be giving the impression of a set, standard presentation when this will put people off. Often it is not credible that something should be regarded as being all things to all people. Everyone wants you to relate what you describe to them individually, not simply go through some seemingly standard 'patter'; thus for the Chairperson there may be many good reasons for people to join their committee, but what may best persuade one individual is a particular selection and arrangement of them.

In all these cases observation may allow you to spot what is happening and to adjust your approach in a way that minimises the problem. If necessary you can jump back to earlier in the conversation: *I get the distinct impression that I haven't explained this very well. What I should have said was ...* This effectively allows you to have a second chance, revisiting part of your explanation and aiming to make it more powerful so that it no longer prompts a but.

So, objections can help keep you on track, they are a sign of interest and can also be an opportunity to impress people by the way you deal with things (not, of course, that you should encourage objections just so that you can impressively demolish them!). When they do occur, however, and they will, there is no reason why you cannot regard them as something routine and something where how you handle them can act to build your credibility as you go along. Well handled they can become final stepping stones en route to the far bank and a successful agreement.

Preventing objections

In many things it is often a sound principle that prevention is better than cure. In objection handling there are two ways in which prevention can help.

The first is in the area of preparation. Few objections should come at you like a bolt from the blue. Most of the topics of objection that occur you will have anticipated if you have thought things through or, with a regular topic, you may well have had to deal with them previously. Specific circumstances create examples: if you are trying to involve someone in charity fundraising and it will involve them in some public speaking, then, given that many people are reluctant to do this, you might anticipate objections on that score.*

You should have thought through the perennial objections you receive or, on a one-off situation are likely to receive, and, although

---

FOOTNOTE: In which case, buy them a copy of *How to craft successful business presentations and effective public speaking* (Patrick Forsyth: Foulsham)! Yes, I have mentioned this before, but if a book about persuasion cannot contain some plugs, what can – and didn't I mention the power of repetition earlier? Well, it enables me to mention that again too.

they will often be phrased in different ways and come with different power and emphasis, you should be ready for them and have various ways of handling them in mind. As and when new, or differently phrased, objections do occur, then you need to think about possible answers to these too and add something about them to your repertoire.

Second, there are objections that may typically remain unspoken. This does *not* mean they are not in people's minds; some will be and these will then go to form part of the balance upon which they will ultimately agree or reject your proposition. Where experience shows that this is likely to be happening, it may be necessary for you to raise the issue yourself in the conversation in order to deal with a specific point and get it out of the frame. This is best approached head on: *You may have been wondering about* ... *let me spend a minute explaining how we can deal with that* ... *You have not mentioned* ... *do you have any questions about that?* And if you have thought through the answer, or at least the kind of answer necessary, then you can deal with the matter and perhaps also make the matter seem reasonably inconsequential.

'Sparring' with objections

We do not demolish objections, we are not even always able to overcome them and we certainly do not want objection handling to develop into an argument. Indeed it is quite possible to win an argument – yet lose the chance of coming to an agreement. If, when someone raises an objection, you immediately allow your hackles to rise and your every response abruptly dashes into the dialogue and starts with the words, *Ah, but* ..., there is every chance that the conversation will become a tad confrontational and that is not conducive to gaining agreement. It is for this reason that you should use the technique known as 'sparring'. Sparring concerns offering an appropriate initial response, and is a useful preliminary to the process of objection handling and providing a satisfactory answer. The sparring can do several things. It acts to make it clear that you:

- •)) Are listening carefully.

- •)) Will initiate no argument.

- •)) Accept the point made and will deal with it rather than deny it.

- •)) Will treat what has been said seriously.

- •)) Do not think the objection is contentious, or unnecessarily demanding.

So, sparring is the process of saying something that positions how you will deal with the objection: *That's a good point, John. I can see I must give you more information in that area ...*, *You are quite right to raise that. It is an important point. Let me ...*, preferably something that includes – or better still starts with – at least a hint of agreement. In this way you can provoke feelings in the objector's mind that will make dealing with the objection easier. This can mean starting baldly with the word Yes, even when you know what you want to do next is persuade someone they are wrong. Because doing so is counter-intuitive, it needs remembering and may also necessitate a conscious effort. However, if you can make someone say to themselves: *Good, there's not going to be an argument* or *They accept the point, now let's see what they have to say about it* then they will be more receptive to what you say next. This principle may be more important than it seems because some objection areas are difficult and can quickly become emotional. Sparring has the effect of 'lowering the temperature' of the conversation prior to going on to provide the answer.

There is another important result of using this technique. Sometimes you will get objections that are new, that you are not expecting, not familiar with or that do, if only for a moment, throw you. These can present real difficulty when you feel you have to come back fast with a credible response and leave no hiatus in the conversation. Luckily the construction of the human mind is such that in the time it will take you to say something like: *That's a good point, Mary. We are certainly going to have to satisfy you about that if we're to reach agreement. Let me ...*, then your mind can be doing a great deal of thinking and you may well be on the way to an answer. Sparring builds in a bit of time to think, just when you may need it most; and very useful that can be too, especially as it allows it to happen without pointing up the fact that you need it. It sets up a situation that is as favourable as possible to dealing with the objection itself, and makes it more likely that you can do so effectively.

But ultimately you still have to answer the point made.

Providing an answer

Never attempt to deal with an objection until you have sufficient information as to exactly where someone is coming from as the basis of your answering. If you assume wrongly exactly what is meant or treat a serious point superficially, you will quickly be in trouble and likely to make matters worse. Objections must not be allowed to put you on the defensive. Sparring helps set the scene. Two other initial responses are also well worth bearing in mind.

First, never be afraid to respond to a question with a question of your own. This will be understood and accepted: after all, how can you be expected to comment sensibly about a point until you know exactly what lies behind it? More than one question may be quite acceptable, though you should make it clear what you are doing: *That's a fair point, John. Let me make sure I understand exactly what you mean. Can you tell me ...?*. This is an important point as simple questions or comments may either disguise a deeper point or, more often, can have several possible interpretations. Consider an example in a sales situation. A customer comments on price (they so often do!) saying something like: *That is very expensive*. What do they mean? It is a comment, not even phrased as a question and could mean many things. For instance, it could mean:

•)) *It is more than I expected.*

•)) *It is more than I pay now.*

•)) *It is more than another quote.*

•)) *It is over my budget.*

•)) *That cost is beyond my authority to decide.*

•)) *I'm not convinced it is value for money.*

•)) *Will you negotiate?*

•)) *I'm not clear what I get for it.*

•)) *It is a lot to pay at once.*

•)) *I don't understand.*

•)) *No.*

•)) *Can the (product) specification be reduced to cut costs?*

•)) *I will have to think about that.*

•)) *I cannot decide now.*

There could be more such meanings. Clearly many of these interpretations will need answering along different lines; it makes the point clearly that you always have to understand exactly what is meant before you deal with it. This is true of so many things: persuading someone to serve on a committee might well get them saying, *I can't afford the time.* But that too needs qualifying: at present/on the regular meeting day? Or maybe it is just a polite way of putting you off – if someone cannot drive and is worried about the journey to the meeting, they may avoid the issues that raises. Even the busiest person might be prepared to rearrange things to some extent if they feel it is worthwhile.

Second, if something is thrown out as a comment or challenge, just like, *But that is very expensive* in the above example, and it is in a form that is not a question, then you can often turn it back to the questioner as a question designed to clarify. Thus: *But that is very expensive* could be followed by the question: *Yes, Mary, it is a considerable cost, though I would suggest, of course, it is a good investment. But what exactly are you saying? Is it more than you had budgeted for?* This kind of approach does a number of things quickly:

- •)) It acknowledges the point (here there is no merit in denying it is a great deal of money if they clearly feel that it is; indeed, there is no merit in any argument that is merely about personal and subjective judgements).

- •)) Suggests you will be happy to discuss it.

- •)) Makes asking for more information about their concern seem helpful.

Once these preliminaries are out of the way, you can move on to actually address the objection. If you continue to keep in mind the image of a balance (described earlier) and bear in mind that there will be points – of varying importance and weight, on either side – then the job you must do here is one of ordering the balance, or reordering the one you have described, so that – despite some objections – it still presents a favourable basis for a positive decision. Often, of course, people are not going to automatically agree if the balance is positive; they are only going to agree if your described balance stacks up better than those of any alternative which they may also be evaluating.

Ultimately, as you answer objections, you have only four options that you can use in rebalancing, so at least mechanistically there is no great complication here.

- •)) **Remove them:** The first option is to remove the objection, to persuade the person that it is not actually a negative factor. Often objections arise out of sheer confusion, for example when the presenting partner said that – *I don't have time for a full rehearsal!* – this might be based on an overestimate of how long it will take. Tell them what you have in mind is an hour or so, and not the whole morning they envisaged, and the objection evaporates.

•))) **Reduce them:** Alternatively you can act to show that although there is a negative element to the case, it is a minor matter – *getting this presentation right is so important. It will take a moment certainly, but surely an hour or so is worthwhile?*

•))) **Turn them into a plus:** Here you take what seems like a negative factor and show that it is, in fact, the opposite – *rehearsal seems elaborate and it will take an hour or so, but we both have to do some individual preparation. Rehearsal will halve that time and ensure the presentation goes well.*

•))) **Agree:** The last option, and one that the facts sometimes make necessary, is to agree that an objection raised *is* a snag – *you're right, it is time-consuming, but this presentation has to go well and there is no other option.*

As these are the only alternatives, once you have decided if the objection is real or imagined, you simply have to choose what suits you best in a particular case. In all cases, especially perhaps the last, your answer can link back to benefits, touching again on points made earlier in a way that can act as a summary and prompt people to consider the whole balance rather than one point in isolation.

The problem of money

We are all sensitive about money. We do not want to be ripped off, we love a bargain and generally want to be sure that any figures that are suggested to us make sense. In the business world, careful description of price will minimise the incidence of price objections; careful handling of them will remove what can often be a major obstacle to agreement. For those readers who find it relevant, this is worth a separate word. So skip on if you like, though the principles involved here could be applied to other objections that involve figures and money. Even at as simple a level of persuading someone to join a theatre trip or go for a celebratory meal, the question *How much?* may well crop up.

Certainly in selling situations, of all the things that come up as objections price is often the most frequent and the most difficult. Of course, everyone wants value for money, and in many areas they will negotiate to get it if they can. Negotiation is a skill and set of techniques in addition to that of selling: if selling – persuasion – obtains agreement, then negotiation agrees the details of that agreement. This is beyond the scope of this book, though I have written on this in *Successful Negotiating* (How to Books); the quotation at the start of the first chapter gives a feeling for the process. Annabel (aged six): *If you want a guinea pig, then you start by asking for a pony.* At the least, customers want to assess value for money and often to compare what is offered in this respect with competition or other options. So how can this be handled? Let us continue to focus on sales situations here for a moment more. First, the way someone positions a statement of price has an effect on the likelihood of subsequently receiving price objections. Price should rarely be dealt with in isolation. By describing it alongside benefits, you can make it speak much more of value for money. This certainly applies for any factor likely to be contentious.

Sales people must beware also of presenting price so that it runs foul of the way in which people regard money psychologically. Here are some examples:

·)) **Avoid price barriers:** We all see things priced at sums like £9.99 in many retail outlets, and somehow this is perceived as being significantly less than something at £10. Similarly with higher amounts, £4995 seems less than £5000, a house priced at £199,500 is set below the nearest round figure (and tax thresholds complicate this). This may seem silly to you, we all *know* such figures are virtually the same thing as the round figure above them, but there is a great deal of research to back up the psychological response to such things – the lower price really does mean agreement to buy is more likely. I suggest you do not worry about why, but use the fact where you can.

•)) **Amortise the price:** This is the technique of quoting a figure of, say, £1000 (or around a thousand) per month, which seems less than £12,000 over a year. This can be used in a variety of ways to split larger figures down, spreading them over different budgets, people, or time frames. The amounts do not have to be large: if the Chair wants to persuade someone to join the writing group I attend, they do not say that attendance costs more than £50 a year, rather that it is *only a pound a week* (and you get, in my case, two cups of tea for that!). Additionally, any way of stressing the economies of scale is also part of this.

If you have more flexibility in setting prices, as is the case with those selling a tailored service (as I do in training), for example, then:

•)) **Judge the price range carefully:** To say something will be between £4000 and £7000 may seem too vague, whereas £4000–£5000 or even £5500 may be acceptable as a first ballpark figure. A second point here, always be careful about the highest point of a range. Quote something you then exceed and the perception of you changes for the worse and does so fast: *These people always go over their estimate.* Coming in below an estimate helps ensure people are sufficiently satisfied to come back to you next time.

•)) **Avoid round figures:** When quoting bespoke arrangements, as is again the case with consultancy and fees, with the work based on the client's unique brief, it will not be credible if it comes to a round figure like £10,000. If it does, people will assume that this is an impossible coincidence and probably assume also that you have worked out a figure and then rounded it up.

Finally here, a useful way to remember some good phraseology when dealing with price can be hung round the four mathematical symbols:

+   mention: this **plus** .../in **addition to** ...

−   mention: ... **reducing** costs/**eliminating** the need for .../ **lessening** this .../**minimise** ...

×   mention: ... something producing **multiple** advantages or opportunities/**enhanced** service/... **greater** productivity/ **more** satisfaction

÷   mention: **amortise** costs over ... /**spread** across .../**divided** between .../**apportioned** to ...

This is a simple mechanism, one useful in any context where you must deal with money matters and emphasise value.

As a last word on this: perhaps more than anywhere else, objections based on price or money factors in all their manifestations are things for which you must be ready. Prepare well and deal with them with authority and confidence and you will find you can handle them.

Do not knock alternative choices

Where what is happening is that someone must decide not simply whether they do this or not, but whether they do this or something else, you may well be aware of this fact. If you want someone to spend time on rehearsing a presentation, an example used earlier, and they say they have a report to finish writing, immediately suggesting that doing so is not important will not be likely to go down very well. So do not knock alternatives. This is certainly good advice for someone selling a product or service (here the alternatives are competitors). Sometimes sales people will be asked outright about competition: *What about firm X?* Or: *We also plan to talk to company Y. Do you know them?* If you are in this position, two responses are to be avoided:

•))) **Do not single them out:** *Yes, I know them. They are my biggest competitor.* Such a response is likely to make the buyer think they should check them out.

•)) **Do not knock them:** *I certainly know them. I thought everyone knew the trouble they are having in the market at present.* It is a way of life that at that point they declare that they have done business together very satisfactorily in the past, or that there is some other connection that makes such a knock particularly inappropriate. Besides, it is very difficult not to let such comments sound like sour grapes.

A more constructive response is called for, something like: *There are a dozen or more competitors for us in this sector, we come across them all and each has certain strengths.* This makes checking them all out seem complicated, and while giving no detail, does acknowledge that you know they are also good. It is also a more credible response.

Exactly the same kind of thing may occur away from business. If you are fundraising for a charity, you may find people are reluctant to contribute because they say, *I already support X.* Try to persuade your son to mow the lawn and you will not get far by knocking the things (many things no doubt) that he has to do that prevent it. Acceptance that the other things are important may well be a better starting point and then the job is to show reasons why this chore should be fitted in despite that (a little more persuasion might save some money here, given the attitude of many teenagers!).

Care in all references to any sort of competitive offering or alternative always pays off. The last thing you want is a protracted argument, prompted by some detailed negative comment you make. Someone may then feel they must defend their position, as accepting it may make their past decision about something else look ill-judged. One last point here, if a 'competitor' is named (and it is something you can do worse than ask about if it is not named) then information about what you are up against may well help you decide on the line you will take. The teenager who is just too busy is much more difficult to persuade than the one who tells you specifically what he feels he should be doing rather than mowing the lawn.

Avoid untenable comparisons

There is an old saying to the effect that while you can compare apples with apples, there is no merit in comparing apples with old shoes. Yet people do the latter all the time. Customers say something like: *That's all very well but I can get the same thing from Firm X on much better terms* to sales people. But what they actually mean is that they can get something *rather different* from elsewhere; otherwise they would surely not be debating the point, they would simply go elsewhere. On that basis they are no doubt correct; there are always many permutations on offer in any particular industry. They seek justification of a particular package or deal, and very often of the price (they may want a discount), in comparison with the quoted alternative – though they rarely elaborate on the details of that other offering.

The answer in such circumstances cannot lie with a direct comparison when, as is most often the case, the two things are *not*, in any case, exactly the same. This is true of many situations: someone might contrast spending time on a committee by saying *I can spend the time just as usefully in another way.* But it will not be the same. A sales person's quoted competitor may be less costly, but the specification may also be less, the quality lower, fewer ancillary items may be included, associated costs may be higher, credit terms or guarantees may be different, design details may vary, delivery or timing may be longer or less certain. The possibilities are many.

A persuasive response must identify and then deal with these differences. The first answer may well be, Yes, you can get *something similar* elsewhere (do not deny it; that way lies fruitless argument) *but it is certainly not identical, in our discussions you have emphasised the need for reliability, our ...* and go back to the specific benefits you have identified they want. In some circumstances your first response may need to be a question; you have to find out more about what is being offered to discover how in fact it differs from your offering. In terms of the price of a product, if one is more expensive then the additional amount over and above a competitor's can only be explained and justified by reference to the gap between what the two parties offer; in other words, what does the extra amount of money buy? Does it provide better service, higher quality or what? Or indeed what would paying less lead them to miss, for you can discuss it both ways round. Identifying and dealing with this gap is the route to answering any objection that comes up from this sort of lead in.

People certainly want value for money, they also want a 'good deal', but they will not sacrifice key requirements for savings or reductions in other factors (quality etc.) that may prove to be a false economy. It is a fact that many of the most successful products and services in many markets are not the cheapest; just look at the big-name products in supermarkets. Cost and quality go together and so if money is involved in what you are doing you should describe your quality or 'value' with confidence; it is what justifies the cost. Avoid odious and inappropriate comparisons, which people may make only to antagonise, or as an opening to negotiation, and make sure that, regardless of what someone else may do, you only ever compare apples with apples.

Use the 'boomerang' technique

Something else that can be useful in handling objections is a particular form of words, which turns an objection back on itself so that the question posed links to the answer. Thus:

> John: 'As you know this is now very urgent, I don't know that we have time for …'

> Mary: '*It is because I know you want things sorted out fast, John, that I am suggesting this. It will not take long and could avoid more significant delays if you went ahead without and hit any snags.*'

If the topic here is linked to something that someone rates highly, such as needing something urgently, then this kind of response can get you back on track away from the difficulties and apparently focusing on exactly what they see as important. This technique constitutes a manner of presentation that can make someone feel that what they regard as the key issue is genuinely being acknowledged, and that the answer is being dealt with in a way that addresses it.

Excuses

Let us be honest, sometimes people disguise their reasons for not acting as we wish. They say – *it will take too long* – *the cost is too great* – or whatever else when they are simply being stubborn or are unwilling for whatever reason to say exactly what they think (and this could be to save your feelings!). In this case you need to try to recognise what is an excuse and what is not. A long justification of time or cost will achieve nothing if that is only a disguise for the real reason. For example, say your fellow presenter said they did not like the thought of presenting with you. Maybe what they are saying is that they are not very confident of their presentational skills and do not want you to witness or surpass them.

Suspect something like this is going on and the only way forward is to ask questions, and perhaps to drive things out in the open – *Be honest, that's not really an issue. Why do you really object?*

Saving face

Sometimes people's objections prove false. Something makes them challenge some point when actually the facts are entirely on your side and the balance is good and positive. The temptation in a hectic meeting, especially one in which a fair number of objections have been raised, including perhaps some difficult ones, is to heave a sigh of relief that one is mistaken and blurt out the equivalent of *You're wrong!* This is a natural reaction but can result in the instigator of the point being made to feel bad, or worse, feeling they have been made to look silly. Clearly this is something to be avoided if good relations are to be maintained.

There can be many reasons for people to be mistaken; an original impression about something you have told them may be wrong: out of date perhaps. They may have misheard something or misinterpreted something they read, or it could be your fault – you may have put something over badly, not gone into sufficient detail, gone on talking while their attention was elsewhere; or you may not know where the fault lies; indeed, it may not matter.

What is important here is to let people down lightly. Suggest that it is an easy or commonly made mistake. This may still leave them feeling somewhat bad. It may be better than this to suggest you are at fault, albeit in a general and unspecified way: *Sorry, perhaps I gave you the wrong impression about that. The fact is .... If I was insufficiently clear about that, I apologise. It is not, in fact, a problem; the fact is ....* This works well in either case. Sometimes people know, or realise, they are at fault and rather like an approach that avoids laying blame or making them feel bad about it. Sometimes it is no one's fault, but the approach is still seen to be sensitive. Just a little care in this area can get over what otherwise can be small upsets to the smooth progress of the conversation and the development of a positive case. You should not overdo it, or it will risk sounding patronising, but do avoid drawing attention to errors.

This whole area – the smooth, assured handling of people's objections – is an important one to get to grips with. Not least it avoids there being any hiatus between the presentation of a strong case and the next stage, now reviewed in the next chapter, of obtaining a firm, positive commitment.

> **Regarding objections as an opportunity, anticipating what objections may be made and in what form they will come, and then dealing with them neatly, must be an inherent part of being persuasive. Simply putting over your case well is never enough. Because of human nature and the way in which people make decisions you are guaranteed to receive some objections. Being ready for them, dealing with them and ensuring that the balance people are building up in their minds remains positive will keep you on the path towards getting your own way.**

CHAPTER 6

Gaining a Commitment

We cannot ensure success, but we can deserve it.

John Adams
US President

It is perhaps primarily the need to 'close' (the jargon word used for completing the sales process to secure agreement) that sets persuasive communication apart from other more straightforward kinds of communication. It can involve getting the other person to make a decision, change their minds or even upturn the habits of a lifetime. As such it can present problems. The whole process is psychologically difficult in some senses for whoever is doing the persuading, holding out as it does the prospect of success – or failure and a lack of agreement. Furthermore people sometimes find it difficult to make a decision. It is a stage that is dependent on what has gone before, but it is also one that must occur of itself. If you cannot or will not close and handle that stage well, perhaps through a fear of rejection, then your overall effectiveness will always be less powerful than it might otherwise be. Here we review this crucial stage.

Your own commitment to close

Closing a deal is the ultimate objective of all persuasion. Sometimes the nature of a particular persuasive process means that you can reach it in stages, in which case you effectively have to close a number of times, on all the interim commitments on the way of which there can be many. It may represent a close to get someone to say a number of things, for example:

•)) *Yes, I'll meet with you.*

•)) *Yes, send something* (perhaps some documentation).

•)) *Yes, let me have a detailed proposal.*

•)) *Yes, let's meet again to take things further.*

•)) *Yes, I agree* (the ultimate decision).

The final attempt to gain a commitment is less a full stage of the process (in the sense of the time it takes); rather it is just a phrase or, more often, merely a question. You have to know when to ask such a question and you have to actually do it. Closing can be a weak area with some persuaders, one that allows previous good case making to be wasted as agreement is not made to conclude the process; indeed, little or nothing is done to prompt it. Though that may be less because it is done badly, than because it is not done at all. Some – most? – people, understandably, dislike it when people say *No* – and in some circumstances this may not be said politely. So people are tempted and may find themselves taking a safer route to ending a conversation. They say things like: *I hope this has been useful – I hope I have been able to give you all the details you need at this stage – Is there anything else I can add before we finish?* This kind of non-close finish almost guarantees a pleasant end to the meeting, with people responding with statements such as: *That's been very useful, thanks very much for talking to me – You've given me all the information I need at this stage. Thank you very much for your time.* All very nice, everyone likes to feel they have been helpful and everyone likes to receive thanks; but such responses are usually followed by one other little word: *Goodbye*, drawing matters to an end before a commitment has been made and before any follow-up action can be arranged.

So resolve to close – to actually ask for agreement. You have to be thick-skinned about any rejection; even the most persuasive people do not have a one hundred per cent strike rate, so there will always be some negative conclusions. But if you aim to close every time at every stage then, along with a little rejection, you may well get more successful agreements than those who approach it in a more faint-hearted manner.

Watch for signals that a decision is imminent

The advice is often given that the best time to go for a commitment is at the earliest time possible. This is a little glib, but there is some truth in it, to the extent that you can leave things too late and allow the moment to pass. Certainly you need to watch for signs that someone is ready to make a decision. Left alone some people are very indecisive, or at the least they will take a long time to make up their minds. This may be for constructive reasons, and you must be wary of trying to shortcut the weighing-up factors, which they see as making a sensible decision possible; people are very wary of being rushed into something. But if the delay is just out of what some people might see as a perverse desire to delay, then closing may act as a catalyst to prompt a decision.

Remember, this final stage does not cause people to agree; only the power of persuasion from the picture you have built up and the case you have put over can do that – by creating the interest that closing then converts into becoming a positive agreement. So the final kind of feedback you need during a persuasive conversation is in the form of what (in selling) are called 'buying signals'. These signals of agreement are less easy to define than to spot. Some will be in the form of a series of signs of interest, expressions, comments, noises even, nods certainly, all of which indicate satisfaction with what is being presented. The most tangible sign is probably comments about the situation that will pertain *after* agreement, for example: *Then after we have (done this) we can ... – Once this stage is out of the way we will* .... Such comments may well be interspersed with questions and other signs that some portion of the decision is still to be made. Finally the questions may only be for reassurance; in the person's own mind they have made the decision – and closing merely confirms it and brings it out in the open.

You will come to trust your judgement in this area and it is well worthwhile to make a mental note of what signals you feel you see, and whether they provide an accurate indication of how things went on from there on, as a guide for the future.

Obtaining feedback from a 'trial close'

It is important to realise that closing is not a one-shot situation. Some encounters involve a number of closes: with, for instance, the first rejected but the last agreed. One method of closing that may be used specifically to obtain feedback early on in a conversation – often with no real hope of actually closing at the point it is used – is the so-called 'trial close'. This can really be any kind of close in terms of technique: you may be pretty sure the answer will be a *No*, but the way you phrase things can be designed to give valuable clues as to how near you are getting to acceptance or on what element you should now concentrate to complete the process. For example, if you attempt to close, the response might be someone saying something like: *Now wait a minute. We still need to discuss X,* and you know to move on to discuss just that. This is a useful technique and can provide an alternative way of obtaining very focused feedback at this crucial point in the conversation.

How to prompt final agreement

As has been said, this is less a stage, but perhaps more a simple question or comment. All you need is a particular choice of phraseology to match an individual and the circumstances. There are many permutations, but the most often used are perhaps the following (shown here linked to our running example about joining a committee):

Direct request

This would be just a straight question, for example: *Shall we go ahead and put you on then?*

Requests like this should be used where the person likes to make their own decisions.

Command

This effectively says: *Do this,* perhaps linking it to what logically follows: *With that done you can* ... So, here: *Put the next meeting date in your diary and we'll include you from then on.* This is effectively an instruction, so must be used with some care.

This can be used where someone:

•)) Has difficulty in making a decision; or

•)) Has considerable respect for you.

Immediate gain

For example, *You said you were free on 27th, so if you can give me the go-ahead about joining today, I can make sure that you get all the necessary papers well ahead of your first meeting.*

This could be used where, by acting fast, someone can get a particular benefit, whereas delay might cause certain or severe problems: here deciding today makes it easy to attend the next committee meeting date. The 'hard' version of this is the so-called fear close (below).

Fear close

As in something like: *Unless you decide today, you will miss the next meeting date,* followed by stating the penalties of delay. This is a more powerfully phrased version of 'immediate gain', and should perhaps be used with some discretion.

Alternatives

This is what is called the 'yes' or 'yes approach'. For example, *Do you want to attend on Tuesday next week, or would next month's meeting suit better?* A *Yes* to either gives you agreement. If necessary you can go on to pose alternatives should a first one not achieve what you want. So, in this case perhaps: *Would you like simply to join or come along informally to one meeting to check us out?* (Incidentally, this technique always reminds me of the reply I got on a sales workshop for the sales team at a large hotel when I asked a delegate to give me an example of an alternative close. They said, *That's when you say, 'Are you going to book here or at the Holiday Inn?'* Not the right answer! But I digress).

This method could be used where you are happy to get a commitment on any one of the possible alternatives.

'Best solution'

This combines a question with recapping key issues, usually benefits. For example, *Once you are a member of the committee you will find it's interesting and worthwhile, and that the time commitment really is manageable. Can you attend a first meeting on Tuesday week?*

This should be used when there is any complexity or when a number of different issues are in play; it is also appropriate when the other person is considering more than one way forward.

Question or objection

For example, *If I can persuade you that the time commitment can be kept under control, would you give it a go?*

This should be used where you know you can answer the objection satisfactorily.

Assumption

For example, *Fine. I've got all the information I need to get you on the committee. Once I get back to my desk I'll send you the minutes of the last meeting, and agenda for the next, and all you have to do is be there on the day!*

In other words, we assume the person has said *Yes* and continue the conversation on this basis.

Concession

Trade only a small concession to get agreement now or agree to proceed only on stage one. For example, *If you agree to join, I will guarantee that you do not collect any chores that involve writing. I know you spend so much time doing that already. How about it?*

Some further examples linked to getting a presentation rehearsed are set out in the boxed paragraph on page 128.

Examples: going for agreement

A final phrase to organise the presentation rehearsal might include such as:

- •)) Just ask (*Shall we put a time in our diary?*).

- •)) Tell them, you may not have the authority to instruct them, but make it sound like an order (*Put something in your diary*).

- •)) Suggest why it is a good idea to commit now rather than later (*Let's set a date now, while we can find a mutually convenient time that does not disrupt anything else too much*).

- •)) Suggest why it is a bad idea to leave it (*Unless we set a date now, we will never find a convenient time before the presentation date*).

- •)) Suggest alternatives, positive alternatives where agreement to either one gives you your own way (*So, shall we clear an hour for this or make it two?*). And repeat as necessary (*So, an hour it is then, this week or next?*).

- •)) Assume agreement and phrase the request accordingly (*Fine, we seem to be agreed. Let's get our diaries out and schedule a time*).

In every case, firmly done and at a good moment.

However you decide to phrase things, and whatever kind of close you select and use, the key thing here is to take the initiative and actually initiate a conclusion. You need to do so firmly, and do so more than once if necessary and do so with everyone at every stage of the process.

Finally to end this chapter let me quote American business guru Tom Hopkins: *It's the winning score, the bottom line, the name of the game, the cutting edge, the point of it all ... unless you can close, you're like a football team that can't sustain a drive long enough to score. It's no good if you play your whole game in your own territory and never get across the goal line. So welcome to the delightful world of closing. If you don't love it now, start falling in love, because that's where the money is.* He was laying it on a bit thick because it is important. But a focus on getting whatever agreement you are after must pervade everything you do and, not least, it must ensure that you finish what you do in a way that gives you the best possible chance of success. He is not just talking about technique; he is also talking about motivation. Successful persuaders *want* to succeed, they aim to succeed and are prepared to see the thing right through, despite the risk of a proportion of encounters ending in rejection.

As a final word at this point, having reviewed the sequence of a meeting or conversation, let us dwell for a moment on the totality of one case that has been briefly referred to as we have progressed (see boxed paragraph on pages 130–131).

There is more. Of course, at this stage, especially if you have been handling matters well, all may be finished. Yes, they say and agreement is made. Sometimes this will happen, but sometimes it will not: hence the next chapter.

Asking for a pay increase

This is a matter of persuasion if anything is. It is also one where it is very easy to let your personal feelings swamp any attempt at putting an objective argument.

So first, some do's and don'ts:

Do not say: *I've been working very hard, I have been here a long time, X got more money so I should too.* Do not quote a friend in another organisation and never plead poverty due to personal circumstances that have nothing to do with work (*I'm moving house, having a baby, planning a special holiday*). Also do not threaten, demand or become emotional.

Over and above maintaining an ongoing payment level (due to inflation) there may be good reasons for a rise, so *do* say if you have:

- •)) Increased your responsibilities or the breadth of your operational area in some way.

- •)) Saved the organisation money.

- •)) Worked longer or more unsociable hours than in the past.

- •)) Travelled or stayed away from home more.

- •)) Achieved new qualifications or skills.

- •)) Become more self-sufficient.

- •)) Increased your contribution (with ideas, for instance), especially if you can document results coming from that.

- •)) Exceeded expectations or targets in terms of tangible results.

Fit your request with any prescribed review processes where possible, but then, or whenever you need to push, do so confidently and assertively (the worst answer you will receive is perhaps *No*, in which case plan – agree? – when you can best ask again). As long as you do not ask every five minutes, no one will resent you asking, especially if you make a good case. An agreement to look at the situation in three months could be a satisfactory first result. Additionally, you probably need to be prepared to respond to something that appears to be other than the final offer or response – negotiation may be another technique you need to deploy here (and which is another useful career skill that has been mentioned).

Provide proof: statistics ranging from national figures to more local ones may be useful, as may a note about past discussions, especially any promises made.

Be objective, be factual – and stay calm.

Always document what happens carefully (for your own record or for your boss) and keep such in a safe place. As a final thought here: a creative approach might work. In an idle moment a boss of mine once told me he had himself obtained a pay rise by saying he would have to work harder that year as it was a leap year. I waited more than two years until the next one to remind him – and delivered a moment of amusement and got a small, extra, increase as a result!

No one will make a good persuader if they fail to 'close'. Recognise the right moment, select the best way to ask for or obtain a commitment and you will always achieve a better rate of strike than those who take a more circumspect approach.

CHAPTER 7

Follow-through Action

Perseverance capitalises inspiration.

Alex F Osborn
Advertising manager and author

If you are at the end of a conversation and agreement has been reached, then there may be no more to do, at least for the moment. But perhaps the conclusion is not the conclusion you want and, while someone is not saying *No*, they are not saying *Yes* either – so what do you do about the maybes?

A prime indeterminate outcome is described below; it is one that may make you think you know the feeling.

Responding to people who say: *Let me think about it*

People may say a number of things other than *Yes* or *No*, and many people find the most difficult thing to deal with is that little phrase, *Let me think about it.* This is essentially positive, yet if you just walk away from it – helpfully allowing them to do just that – then you may never get another chance to move to agreement. Sometimes people who say this do actually mean, *No.* They may feel that it is an easier and more polite route than just saying, *Get lost.* But you need to know whether to take it at face value or not. So what is your best response? It is often very difficult to think of a reason why someone should *not* think about it (unless perhaps you can contribute pressing reasons to decide at once). So the best route may well be to agree: and not simply to agree but to urge them to think about it. Tell them it is an important decision, tell them they must not make it lightly, tell them they should not be rushed, that they must be certain; however you phrase it, make sure you are clearly on the side of thinking about it. As their expectation is probably something more argumentative, this response is usually accepted and allows you to go further. So then go on to ask why exactly they still need to think about it, or what elements of the decision they feel still need review. Often something is then volunteered at this point. Perhaps there is a particular sticking point, something about the case has been less well made than the rest, or there is some area where more information seems to be needed. Then you can try turning the intention back to more discussion, as in this general example:

> 'Let me think about it.'
>
> *'Of course, it's a big decision, you have to be sure.'*
>
> 'That's right.'
>
> *'You must be sure it's right in every respect. Is there any particular aspect which you need to think about?'*
>
> 'Well, I suppose it's the timescale that worries me most; it would be bound to affect current work.'
>
> *'To some extent, yes. But we can minimise that. Perhaps I didn't explain how we would approach that sufficiently clearly. Can I go over it again before we finish?'*
>
> 'OK. I want to have it all straight in my mind.'

Then the conversation or meeting is under way again and there is no reason why it cannot move on towards another close, which may then be agreed without any further wish to think about it being expressed. The phrase *Let me think about it* is regularly a sign that something – and it may be several somethings, in which case you may be able to get the individual to list them before you suggest more discussion – is still unclear or unresolved.

There is an alternative here, however. Someone may ask for time to think about it not because they need time to think, but for some other reason. Perhaps the two most likely are the need to confer with someone else (are they the real decision maker?), or maybe there is something with which they want to make a comparison and they need time to check out the alternative option. In this case, careful questioning may discover either possibility, or indeed others. Then the action on which you plan to close may change; maybe the first step is to try to organise a meeting with their colleague or whoever else is involved (sometimes they appreciate help with any persuasion that may be necessary, as for example when someone needs to involve say their partner or boss and wants to be sure they do approve). Again we see that the better the quality of the information you find out at every stage, the better position you are in to take things further. Such techniques are not infallible, but if they increase your strike rate even a little they are well worth pursuing, and you may be surprised by how often *Let me think about it* leads not to thinking about it, but to extended discussion and then a – positive – decision.

When they say: *Yes*

Now, let us assume you are going to achieve a good strike rate – think positive! Some of the people you communicate with will agree and you will then end up getting your own way. Then what? Well, the first thing is to thank them. You do not need to grovel, and you need to bear the nature of the relationship in mind, but a thank you costs nothing and may well be both highly appropriate and much appreciated. It is good practice to couple some verbal thanks with the reassurance: *Thanks very much, John. I am sure we will find all this works out well all round.* Then consider any practical points that need to be dealt with at this stage:

- •)) Is there documentation to be completed (some kind of formal deal may involve confirmation, contracts and so on)?

- •)) Do you need a signature?

•)) Is there more information you need (an agreed date, a reference number, an e-mail address so that you can keep in touch)?

•)) Are there points still to be discussed/agreed (especially things running on into the future: once a first stage is passed, what then)?

All such matters must be dealt with in a prompt and businesslike way. You are still on show and it is still possible at this stage for someone to change their mind, or demand to negotiate a different arrangement or simply say, *I've been thinking* and rescind the agreement – something that could negate the result you think you have achieved. So deal with such things promptly and end the conversation. Do not chatter on in a fit of euphoria: many a person has talked themselves out of an agreement again at this stage. Of course, some social chat may well be important; there are deals where both parties regard lunch afterwards as natural. Just be a little careful. Be sure that whoever you are dealing with – who no doubt values their time highly – really wants to extend the dialogue. And decide the objectives of such an extended meeting (especially if it is part of or the start of a working relationship). In formal circumstances, do you drop business, talk no 'shop' and treat it socially, or use it to move on to other topics? It is important to make the other person comfortable in this respect. They may not like it if they planned to use the time constructively and you just talk of golf; or vice versa. Of course, in a home or social context the conversation and contact may naturally continue, but it is still sometimes useful to bear in mind that you have moved on and discourage a revisit to the decision if you feel that might end in a revised decision.

Once you have parted, never fail to double-check that your paperwork or notes are completed. People have been known to forget something vital – a figure or other detail – after a good lunch! There may be occasions where a written thank you might be appropriate too. This can be combined with the business element of an arrangement: for instance a new committee member might get a thank you with the agenda for the next meeting – the first they will attend. Some occasions may need more: a bunch of flowers perhaps.

When you have obtained agreement, then any persuasive communication may be at an end (though it may be the beginning of an ongoing dialogue to hold and develop the relationship with someone); but there is more to bear in mind when things are not clear and longer-term contact is necessary.

Persistence and long-term contact

There is a saying: out of sight, out of mind, and it is worth bearing in mind if you seek to get an agreement which will, it is clear, take some time. The possible time-scale varies a good deal and may sometimes be lengthy. I once maintained contact with a client for almost three years during which I got no work from them at all. I met them once during this time, and we had maybe eight or nine other contacts, which included a variety of forms: I telephoned, wrote letters and e-mailed. Then I got a response – and the single largest piece of work I have booked at one go in fifteen years. The time – very little – it took to stay in touch was insignificant compared with the return. It is good, incidentally, to ring the changes on method in such circumstances, remembering that a telephone call leaves no permanent reminder, a written note can be filed or stuck on the fridge door, and that an e-mail, while being quick and easy to send, can be deleted in the blink of a mouse's eye.

The principle here is an important one, and does not apply only in a business context. Be persistent and be organised in your persistence. Do not let too long go by without a reminder, yet do not become a nuisance either; some careful judgement is necessary here depending on the circumstances and who it is that you are chasing. Because it can be awkward, embarrassing even, to maintain contact like this – *Whatever do I say next?* – the rule should be not to put it off but to be disciplined about planning and making the next contact. What influences that contact and when it is done should be your view of the other person and what is necessary and appropriate for them, rather than simply when it is convenient for you.

With someone you work with or see regularly this may be simple; with someone you know less well it may be difficult, especially if you are getting signals that, rightly or wrongly, put you off going further: you telephone and get no reply or are told, *They're in a meeting* or *They're away* or just *They're busy*. So, apart from gritting your teeth and making yourself make one more phone call or whatever, you may occasionally need to think of something a bit more memorable to do to try to prod someone into action. An example from my own writing work, on a subject not a million miles from what we are considering here, might illustrate the kind of thing I mean.

Following writing a short book for a(nother!) specialist publisher, I was keen to undertake another topic for them in the same format. I proposed the idea and got a generally good reaction to my suggested topic – but no confirmation. I wrote and telephoned a number of times. Weeks turned to months – result, nothing. Always I received a delay or a put off (you may know the feeling!). Finally, when a reminder of the possibility came up yet again from my follow-up system, I felt I had exhausted all the conventional possibilities, so I sat down and wrote the following:

Struggling author: Patient, reliable (non-smoker), seeks commission on business topics. Novel formats preferred, but anything considered within reason. Ideally a text of 100 or so pages, on a topic like sales excellence sounds good; maybe with some illustrations. Delivery of the right quantity of material – on time – guaranteed. Contact me at the above address/telephone number or let's meet on neutral ground, carrying a copy of *Publishing News* and wearing a carnation.

I must confess I hesitated a little over whether to send it (it was to go to someone I had only met once), but at the end of the day I decided it was not too much over the top and printed it out in the centre of a sheet of letterhead, signed and posted it. Gratifyingly an e-mail confirmation came by the middle of the morning on the following day; and said they liked what I had sent – *irresistible*. Incidentally, you can now read the result – *The Sales Excellence Pocketbook:* Management Pocketbooks. As so often here, the proposition had been well received, but circumstances then conspired to delay a response. After all, it is often more important to us to get an agreement than it is for the other person to make it. People are busy and what we regard as a priority may simply go on their back burner; such things then need a nudge and something a little out of the ordinary may do the trick.

Sometimes a less conventional approach works well. You should not reject anything other than the conventional approach; try a little experiment and see what it can do for you. But, above all, having put over a good case, do not let your good work wither on the vine – keep in touch and you make ultimately gaining a commitment more likely.

Talking of unconventional approaches, and at a point when we have reviewed techniques of persuasion along the whole sequence of the kind of meeting or conversation in which they take place, let us end this chapter by suggesting there are occasions when not being persuasive is the most persuasive thing to do!

Make a point of not being persuasive

It is said that modesty is the art of encouraging people to find out for themselves just how wonderful you are; in the same way not being 'persuasive' can sometimes persuade people to go along with you. Certainly in a sales situation, a customer may want and need to do business with and through a sales person, but they may also want expert support and advice from someone that they feel they can trust. Too often they actually believe that this is the last thing they will get, that the sales person is only out for themselves and that if they shake hands with them they should count their fingers afterwards to check they are still all present. Sometimes, however, they find that they feel they really can trust a sales person, and this is true of any persuasive situation.

A number of things can be used to help people come more certainly to that conclusion: not being too 'pushy' and exerting undue pressure, for instance. Another method can be introduced with more positive intent: literally saying that you are not trying to persuade. How do you do this? With phrases such as: *I believe honesty is always best, so let me tell you ... If I were trying to twist your arm, I probably wouldn't tell you this, but let me say ....* You let them see what you might do, in effect making the point you could have made in a more overt manner, and yet apparently avoiding doing so. In a way it doubles the power.

You can even get people focusing more on the techniques of another person trying to persuade them towards some other decision than on what they say, by referring to their techniques specifically: *Now I know John has a clever answer to the objection you raise, but let me be honest, I know it is a problem, but it can be overcome by ...* Next time they see your rival they may well notice what they say on the topic and be inclined to be more suspicious of it than would otherwise have been the case.

Of course, such an approach must not be overused and must always be used carefully or it will certainly sound glib. But a regular feeling of this sort within your conversation can add the feeling to the conviction that you really do put the other person's feelings ahead of pushing them into whatever action you want of them.

Take care with this approach, but remember there are many people that will take some display of modesty as a sign that there is strength, expertise and other good qualities underneath – and who will dismiss any overt brashness as not to be trusted.

Persistence is a prime asset in seeking to improve your persuasive strike rate. The problem, if there is one, is largely psychological: it can seem awkward or even embarrassing to pursue this line. Yet it pays dividends, and with resolve and maybe a little creativity it can work well for turning some of the maybes into agreement when otherwise they might go the other way by default.

The Way Ahead

Everyone lives by selling something.

Robert Louis Stevenson
Novelist, poet and travel writer

We spend much of our lives, both at work and in any social interaction, communicating. Most of the time we may think little about it. But we do notice quickly enough when something goes wrong. Never forget that communication can be inherently difficult. It works more effectively and more certainly when it is thought about, when the message is well considered. This is doubly so if there are any special factors involved, and communicating persuasively – setting out to get your own way – is certainly a greater challenge than simpler forms of communication.

In this book you will have got a flavour of how to be persuasive, and to present a compelling case – one that will give someone reasons to give you your own way. There may be no simple magic formula that guarantees success, but, as we have seen, there are a number of principles and techniques that smooth the way and make getting your own way more likely. While you will never win them all, you should certainly be able to achieve a good strike rate.

At the same time persuasion cannot be deployed 'by rote'. There can be no 'script', and although there are guiding principles, there is no single set way of proceeding that allows you simply to follow the rules on 'automatic pilot' each time. Always remember that the approach you take needs to be decided, case by case, person by person. Similar thinking may be involved in analysing a situation and deciding on the precise approach you will adopt, but what works today with one person is just that. Tomorrow, next week, next year, or with someone else, something different may be needed. And the adaptation might involve changing a word or two, or adopting a radically different approach.

This kind of communication must be approached in an individual way, and as circumstances change – who you are aiming to persuade, how they think and what affects them and so on – the approach needs to accommodate them. Thus we will all spend a lifetime honing our persuasive communication skills, not only to become better at deploying them, but also to better fit them to whatever the current circumstances may demand. Recognising that this is necessary is the first step towards keeping your skills ahead of the game and maintaining an acceptable success rate.

So, practice makes perfect. You need to bear in mind the guidelines set out here and give them a try. If things do not go perfectly at first – no matter. But everything you do should be a step in the right direction. The trick is to learn from your experience, to observe and recognise what went well and what went less well, and adapt your approach as time goes by. The maxim mentioned earlier about practice is attributed to more than one sports person (usually a golfer) – *It's a funny thing, but the more I practise, the more my luck seems to improve* – and it contains a clear truth.

Making success more certain

Of course, as has been made clear, a wealth of detail is involved, but let us conclude with a manageable number of points that, while not negating any others, are important. Overall there are perhaps three. You should:

- ·)) **Prepare carefully:** So much stems from the thought you put in before you even open your mouth. Preparation is key. Make time to do it, make it constructive and everything that follows will be that little bit easier.

- ·)) **Adopt a consciousness of the whole process:** Being aware of the processes, approaches and techniques and how they all fit together is the first step to deploying them in a way that makes for effectiveness. The orchestration of all this may seem difficult at first, but the habit of keeping the overview in mind builds up, especially if you aim that it should, and this quickly begins to make the process easier and more manageable.

- ·)) **Be confident:** If you have thought through what you intend to do, if it is based on sound principles and you know that this is the case, then you can afford to be confident. There is a virtuous circle here. Being confident shows. The case you make is then judged differently. It may seem more credible if you have the courage of your convictions, and if so, then as it begins to work, positive feedback can raise your confidence still more.

If you recognise that all this is possible. If you see the necessity for a considered approach and go about building your case with care and putting it over with precision, then you may well surprise yourself with just how persuasive you can be. If you intended to become more persuasive, then you have just got your own way – on this at least.

SUMMARY

Key Issues

In this last section the purpose is to summarise key elements of the content of the book in a way that highlights what makes for success.

If I knew one key magic formula that always guaranteed getting agreement, I would not be writing this; I would be rich and on a nice beach. But there is, as has been said earlier, no magic formula. There is however a variety of things, techniques, approaches that have a disproportionately important influence on success. Some such have been mentioned throughout the text. Remember that success in getting your own way is largely in the detail, and that the whole process is a fragile one. Here, without intending to sideline other issues, key aspects of what makes for success in being persuasive are reviewed under a list of ten main headings.

1 A rounded approach

This activity must not take place in isolation. It is an inherent part of your relationship with people. Thus as a persuader you must:

•)) Recognise that people see, and experience, your communication in a particular way. For example, they may know something of what you want before you start (for example, from previous conversations, hints, or the minutes of an earlier meeting); they may have checked out possible alternatives, done any sort of checking or even research. They expect what happens through the contact and communications that take place to reflect, maintain and extend any positive profile that you may have projected initially. They expect specific promises made at any stage to be kept. If you've said *I only need ten minutes*, then maybe they will expect that and no more.

•)) Act and talk in a way that gels well with all such activities and messages.

This presupposes that you come to the table with a positive reputation and are seen as a reasonable person to deal with. If not (maybe you need to be persuasive despite a previous falling out), then oil may need to be poured on troubled water ahead of coming to the meat of the matter.

Mismatch here just causes problems and jeopardises potential agreement. If you promise someone further information of some sort and then this does not materialise or is delayed, it will be seen as uncaring or as an inefficiency of both you and any organisation you may represent – and one that does not bode well for what will follow.

If you wear the persuasive hat, you have a responsibility to spot any such occurrences (and they can come from many areas) and communicate about them to ensure they are corrected.

2 Your case must be orientated towards the other person

Persuasion, to repeat, is not something that you do *to* people. It is an interactive process that must, as much as anything, reflect the other side of any relationship. This means specifically that:

•)) People's situation, perspective and needs must be accurately identified. Only if you know something about them, can you deal with them in the right kind of way. Moreover, if you make your case fit them better than any alternative, then this is the very best method of differentiating yourself and what you are trying to achieve.

•)) Approaches must respect the nature and circumstances of the individual on the other end. Are they experienced, knowledgeable (or not), are they worried or confident? Conversations must not just incorporate such information and do so specifically, but also *be seen* to do so. Displayed empathy scores points.

·)) Above all, a persuasive approach must *not* appear
standardised and routine. People must feel you are
interested in *them*, are addressing their specific situation
and that what you say is *for them*, not just what you
always say to everyone.

A me, me, me approach risks creating resistance. So too will being
pushy or patronising. A conscious focus on the other person will help
direct the entire communication in the right kind of way, keeping
what you do acceptable yet giving it bite and giving it an edge.

3 Persuasive communication must reflect the decision-making processes

This picks up from point two. Here what is advocated is not a general
orientation towards others, but rather a reflection of the whole
process that someone is going through in making a decision. In the
same way that in boxing or judo you 'go with the attack', here you will
do better following someone's inclinations (though perhaps
modifying and imparting particular emphasis to them) rather than
fighting against them. The thinking process set out earlier really does
reflect human psychology and thus it constitutes an effective basis on
which to proceed. If you get out of kilter with someone, then, apart
from not seeing the relevance of what you are saying, they will also
resent it.

Consider a classic sales situation, one many readers will have gone
through. When I changed my car recently, I talked to three dealers
(looking at cars in broadly the same bracket). I was not asked a single
question by any of them. Amazing! How can you sell a car if you do
not know whether the potential buyer is married, has children or a
dog, how many miles they drive in a year and more? I was offered lots
of information, but it completely lacked any credibility – it was just
the standard spiel. This is a dramatic example, from real life, but
makes a good point. Surely here the logic dictates that the customer

expects to be asked questions, and, what is more, expects too that what the sales person says will be based on the answers. Similarly, any aspect of the way anyone is intent upon making a decision that is ignored risks failure and increases the likelihood that the customer will mark down what is being done and be unlikely to give their agreement.

4 Persuasion demands preparation

You cannot just wing it. Even the best and most experienced (and professional) persuaders rarely wing it (though they may make it look a little like they do). Success comes from sound preparation. The first rule is simple – *you always prepare*. What actually needs to be done however may vary considerably.

You may only need a couple of quiet minutes before going into someone's office. You may need to sit down with one or two colleagues for a couple of hours to thrash out the best way ahead. You may not be able to prepare (as say when you meet someone by chance and the transaction is immediately underway). In the latter case you still need to be prepared: you can think in advance about the type(s) of transaction that may occur, how you make messages persuasive and be ready for most of them.

You may need to make notes, you may need alternative strategies, or you may want to actually rehearse (for something really important perhaps – a mentor might help you practise how to ask for that pay increase, for instance). You *do* need to do something. Consider exactly what is necessary in every situation, do it and you automatically increase your chances of successful agreement. You cannot predict exactly what will happen, and you still need to be quick on your feet, but you will be better able to cope with whatever may come your way if you are prepared.

5 Persuasion must be delivered in an appropriate manner

Often what is needed is a soft approach: one not lacking in persuasive power, but certainly one not guaranteed to put someone's back up. There is a lot of difference between assertiveness and aggression, and what people refer to as being 'pushy' is always something that raises their hackles and makes resistance more likely. The power – projection – that you bring to bear is important. You need confidence, authority even; certainly, people must believe you have the position, personality and profile to be credible in your chosen role.

Empathy is the other key attribute. You need to see things from other people's point of view and *be seen to do so*. Good empathy balances the powerful approach you want to bring to bear; it softens those techniques that would otherwise be seen as 'hard sell' or pushy and makes what you do acceptable as well as appropriate.

This is especially important when there is an element of advice inherent in what you are doing; for example, a manager might want to persuade someone to do something and suggest how it is to be done. Advice must seem soundly based. It must not simply and obviously be what *you* want and what is best for you. The right blend here is worth working at. Think about how whoever you are in dialogue with might best want you to come over and try to match their expectations to some extent. Do not leave out the edge you want, but remember that if what you do is not acceptable it will quickly be rejected; and people may then give more credence to an alternative.

6 Persuasion must incorporate effective discovery

Persuasion is not just about telling – describing – things to people. Success has at least as much to do with asking questions. So:

- •)) Think about areas to question and plan how to phrase matters clearly (not least so that you can get the information you want quickly and, if a number of questions are necessary, the process does not become like the Spanish Inquisition).

- •)) Establish and agree that questioning is necessary (you do not want it to distract or worry people – the logic of the approach should be clear).

- •)) Listen – as in really LISTEN – to, and note if necessary, the answers.

Then the phrasing of your proposition, indeed the proposition itself, can be tailored around their exact situation. The principle here is the same whether the circumstances only permit a couple of quick questions or if you can take half an hour to really establish details or confirm (or revise) the position that exists: what they want, and *why* they want it. Always good information gathering puts you in a position to make a better, and better targeted, pitch and differentiate yourself (and your organisation too if that is relevant) more easily from others.

7 Persuasion must use memorable and creative description

There is a danger that what is said is, or becomes if you do similar things regularly, routine, repetitive – and dull. You may find that you start to abbreviate a little (because you have heard it all before) and the best possible case is no longer made. Or you find yourself assuming that the merits of what you want to say are so self-evident that you sell them short.

There are principles to be followed here:

- •)) Remember that unexpected clarity (especially if something is expected to be complicated) delights people. You need to communicate and, especially with anything intangible and difficult to describe, to ignite people's imagination. This need for clear description is a real opportunity to shine (and again to differentiate).

- •)) Think about the best way of putting things, and do not let the way you talk about something become stale.

- •)) Keep what you say up to date, correct and fresh and make sure it is in fluent language that the other person is comfortable with and understands (and remember that too much inappropriate jargon can deaden any description).

- •)) Bring what you say to life. Avoid bland language – nothing you offer is just *quite* (or even *very*) *good*. If there is nothing better to say about it why should anyone be interested? Avoid imprecise words – like *flexible* – that attempt to be descriptive but fail. (What does flexible mean, for goodness sake? As you read this book you will notice that this page is flexible.) Work at a description to create something clear and memorable. Consider a general phrase: it is one thing to say something is *sort of shiny* (wet fish?). It may be more descriptive to say it is as *smooth as silk* (which certainly conjures up a more precise image), and better still to use a phrase that is more unmistakable and memorable. I once heard someone on the radio describe something by saying it was, *as slippery as a freshly buttered ice rink*. Wonderful. It is just this sort of use of language that being persuasive demands.

Language is the most powerful personal tool you can use in this context; use it in a well-considered way to get the most from it.

8 A persuasive case must be benefit led

The concept of benefits, and features, was investigated earlier and I will not return to the details here. Suffice to say that this is a crucial aspect of being persuasive – something that again can enhance differentiation – and do so positively. You must always be:

- •)) Clear what the specific benefits of an offering are and able to differentiate them from features (something that needs a little thought and is not as obvious as may be thought at first sight).

- •)) Able to prioritise and describe benefits appropriately in the light of what is known about a particular person – remember, a benefit is a benefit is a benefit, but not all benefits are relevant to everyone (some things are consistent; for instance, with products and services, money saved is certainly always 'a benefit', but cheapest is not always best and for some people intent on maximising quality it may not be a relevant benefit).

- •)) Able to make benefits predominate in the overall conversation and relate what they do to the overall 'weighing up' process that characterises the way people buy.

Benefits should mostly be put early on, or even first, in the sequence of what you say, so that you make your explanation 'benefit led' – tell people what they get, then use features to demonstrate how this is possible. This, coupled with the powers of description mentioned above (point 7 in this summary), makes for a powerful approach at the core of the persuasive process.

9 Being persuasive is a complex process and must be well managed

The biggest overall challenge here is perhaps in the management – orchestration – of the whole process. Each individual stage is essentially manageable. But there can be a great deal going on. Throughout a conversation, certainly one of any length, you have to follow your plan and deal with anything that threatens to lead you away from it. You need to fine-tune what you are doing to accommodate unanticipated factors along the way (and to do that you need to have noticed them!). You must listen, concentrate and judge how you do things as well as what you will do. You must often draw with precision from whatever (sometimes not inconsiderable) body of information relates to whatever you are discussing. Much of this information must be held in your head. Sometimes all this must take place alongside whatever technical expertise your task involves, as would be the case if you tried to persuade someone to utilise a computer for something and they are less sure of it than you.

Understanding what needs to be done is important here. The most persuasive people certainly exhibit a real awareness of the details of the process and how it works. So too is confidence: for example, you may need to have sufficient confidence to say *I don't know*, or to pause and say, *Let me think about that for a moment* (a much better option than jumping in with an ill-considered answer, though it can be awkward to do it).

Beyond this, what helps? Remember the anecdote about the person lost in New York? When they asked how to get to Carnegie Hall, they got a one-word answer: practice. Good advice here too. These are skills we can all spend a lifetime in learning. Furthermore, much of the process is dynamic, having to be kept up to date and varied depending on the circumstances in which it is applied; for instance, just the time available can radically change how you may be able to do something. Recognise that and you are half way to dealing with it.

10 Take a long-term view

Success may follow a quick meeting, prompting a clear agreement. That is nice, but it is certainly not always what happens. As you communicate, and concentrate on the moment, you also have to keep a longer-term view in mind. Let me suggest two degrees of time-scale that need to be contemplated:

- •)) **The immediate aftermath of a meeting:** This is best illustrated by the occasion when interest seems high, but you cannot get past a kind of *Leave it with me* comment. Here persistence pays off. Keep in touch, arrange to contact someone again and do so as many times as it takes. It is easy to lose heart as you telephone and are given excuses – *They're in a meeting*. Ask when it finishes, contact them again and ring the changes in terms of method – ring, write, e-mail. If there really is no prospect of agreement, they will tell you. While there remain possibilities for agreement or collaboration in the future, you need to remain fresh in their mind. Increased persistence can be an easy way of getting your own way, once the ground work has been done.

- •)) **Long-term contact:** After an agreement is successfully made (or not, when it may still be worth re-contacting people), make a plan of ongoing contact and avoid losing touch. If, for example, you want to get someone to help you, while they may not agree, perhaps because another commitment precludes it, this does not mean that they will never be available to help. Nurture what you have; it can pay dividends in the future.

It is difficult, perhaps deceiving, to try to encapsulate a topic such as this briefly. However, I am confident that these ten points make sense. Especially when persuasion is likely to be difficult, the details of the matter become even more important, and what can be gained by careful use of core techniques and of approaches that affect things in key ways, is considerable.

This review sets out specific techniques and also highlights other matters: approaches and attitudes that affect matters along the way. What is needed here is that such are:

- •)) Grafted onto the other stock-in-trade expertise that you use in your life, activities and work, to work alongside your other skills, enhancing your overall approach to communicating rather than replacing it.

- •)) Used in such a way that people continue to see you in a positive light: as reasonable, approachable or whatever else is relevant.

- •)) Applied on a 'bespoke' basis so that what is done is always tailored person by person and meeting by meeting to the individual circumstances of each case. It is too simplistic to think that there are a few, standard persuasive approaches that can be deployed every time in exactly the same way.

Many people initially baulk at the thought of 'being persuasive': *I can't be pushy.* Many people though, in my experience, once they set their mind to it (and what you have to do may demand it), find that persuasive communication techniques can go comfortably alongside their normal reasonable persona. They find that their profile is enhanced, not least by the confidence that knowing what they are doing allows them to display, and that so too are the results that they achieve in securing agreement and effectively getting their own way.

Of course, it is always satisfying when you succeed at something like this. Sometimes what is wanted is achieved easily. But most circumstances need the right approach to be carefully deployed if agreement is to be forthcoming. It is then even more satisfying when you succeed and you can look back, sometimes at a long complex chain of events, and say, *I made that happen.*

Now, hopefully with some ideas drawn from here in mind, you can do just that. I have made it clear that luck is not the most important thing here, so I will not wish you good luck, but I wish you well with it.

When I am reasoning with a man, I spend one third of my time thinking about myself and what I am going to say; and two thirds thinking about him and what he is going to say.

Abraham Lincoln
US President

Index